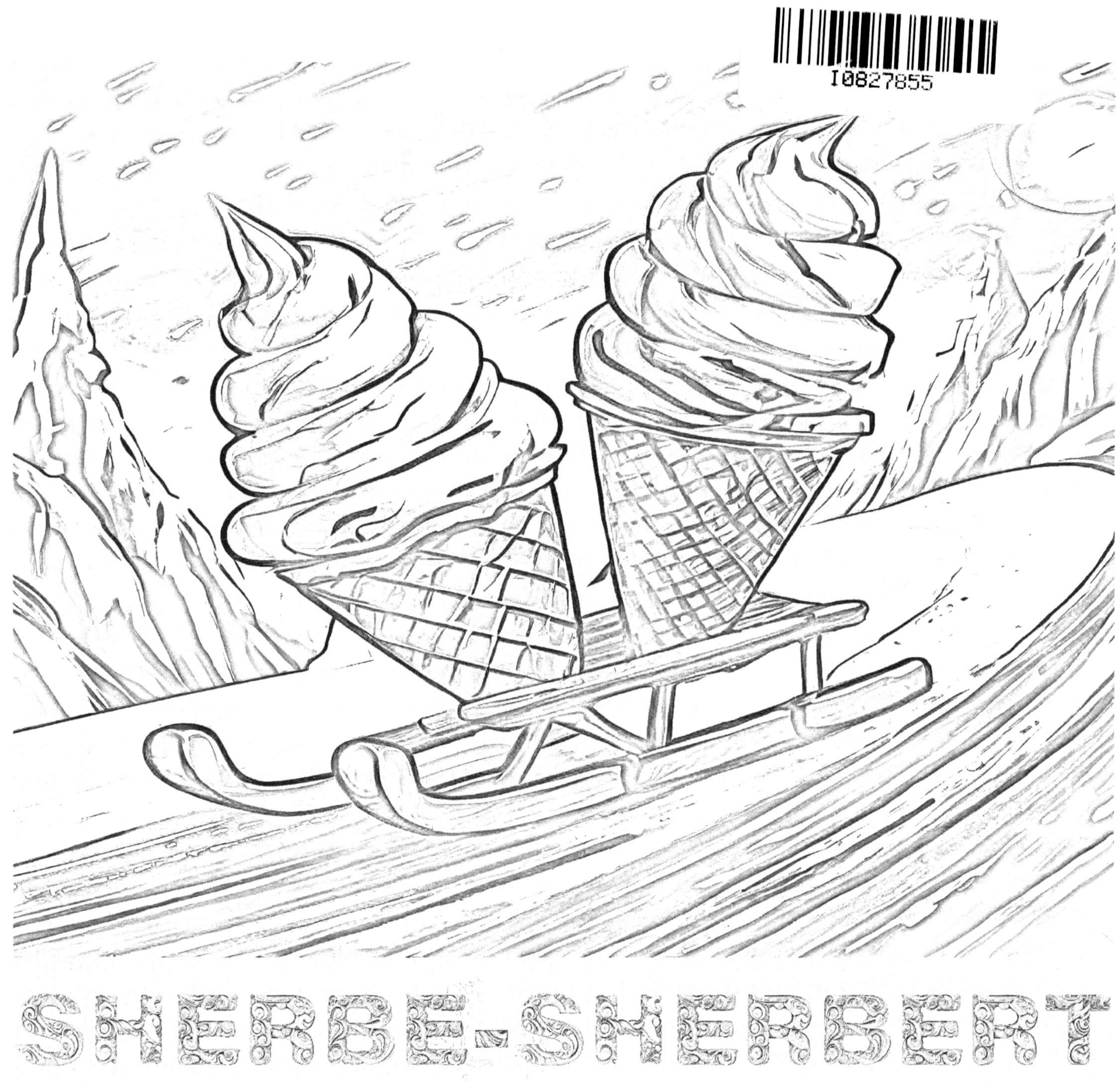

ISBN: 979-8-9902578-2-5

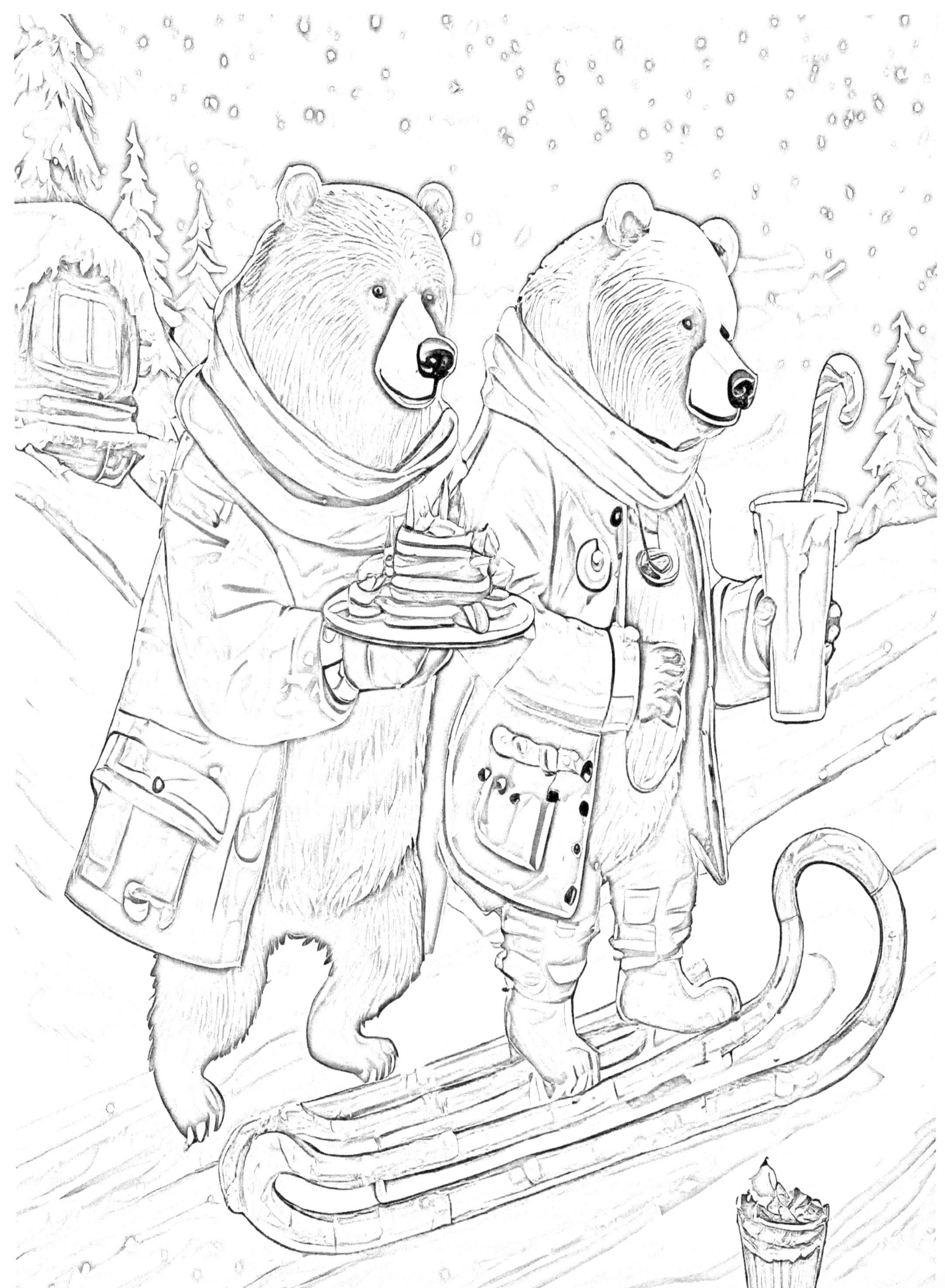

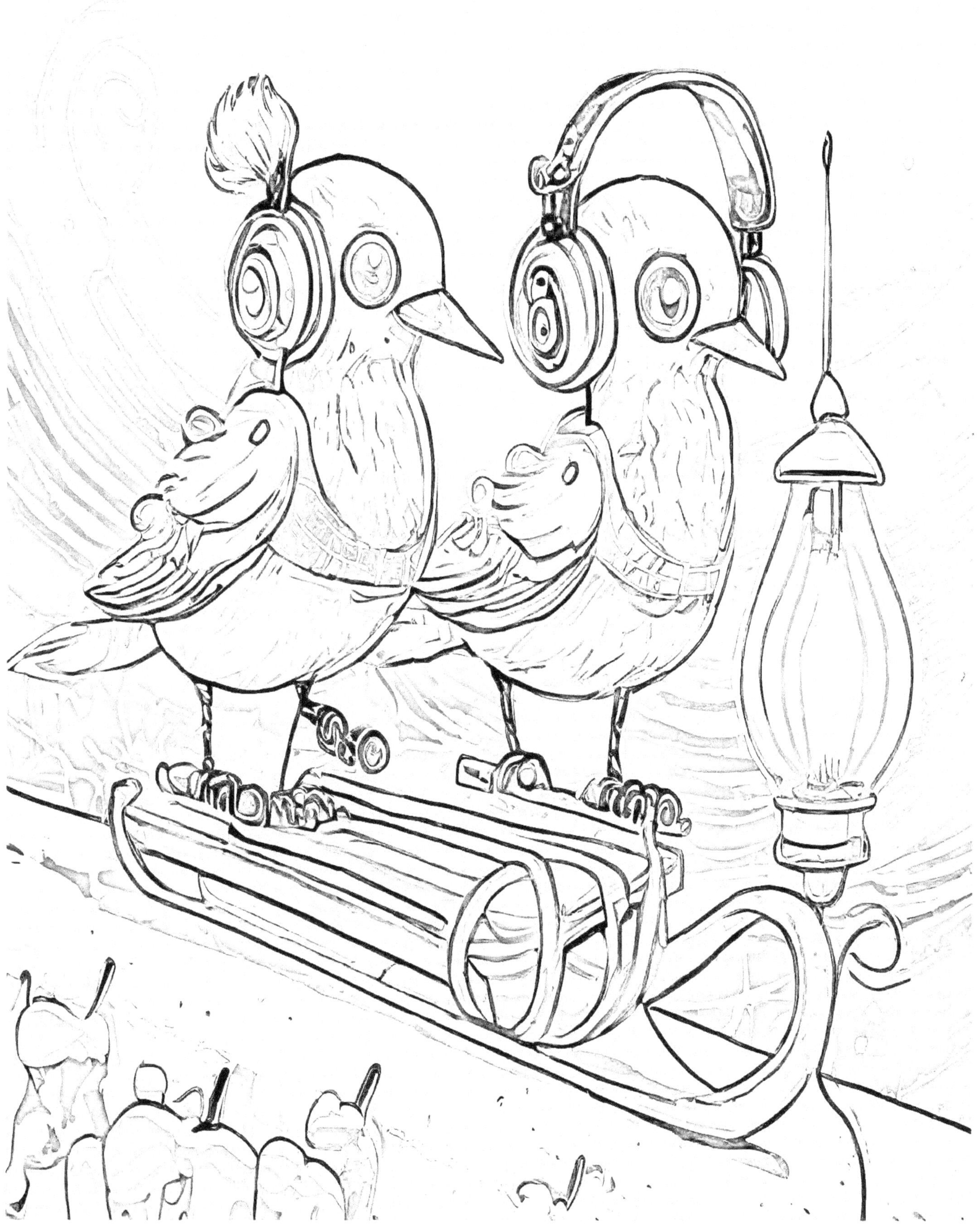

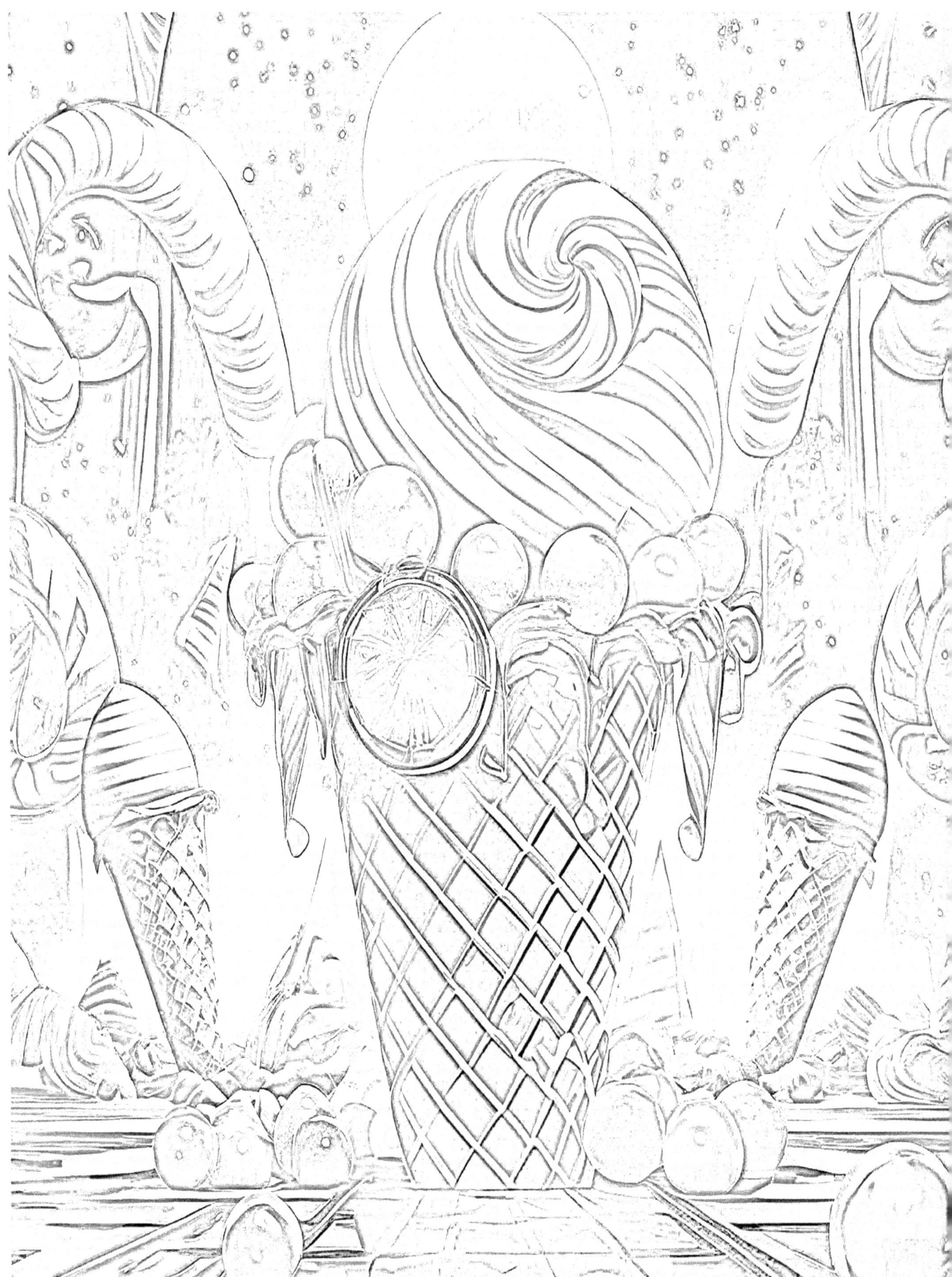

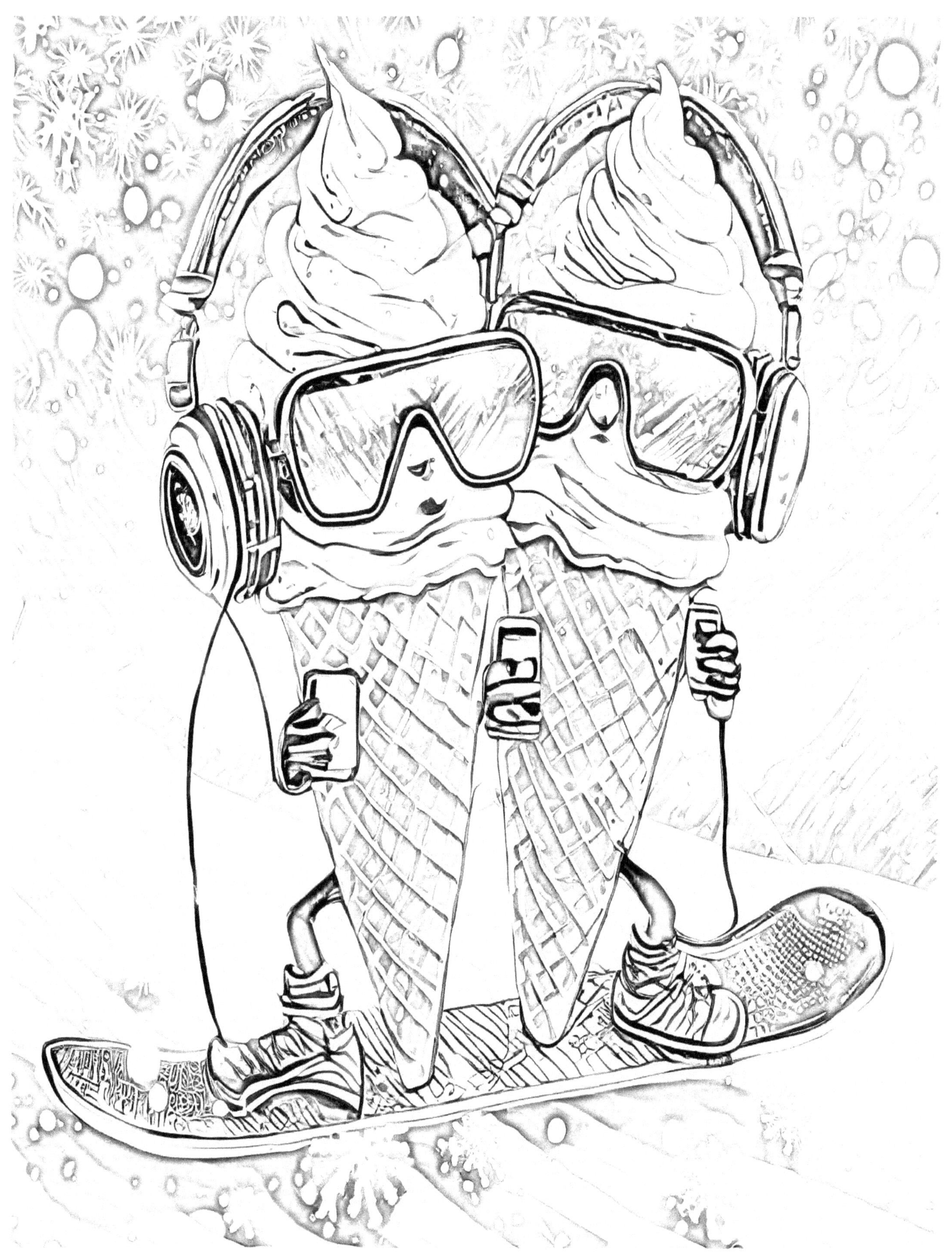

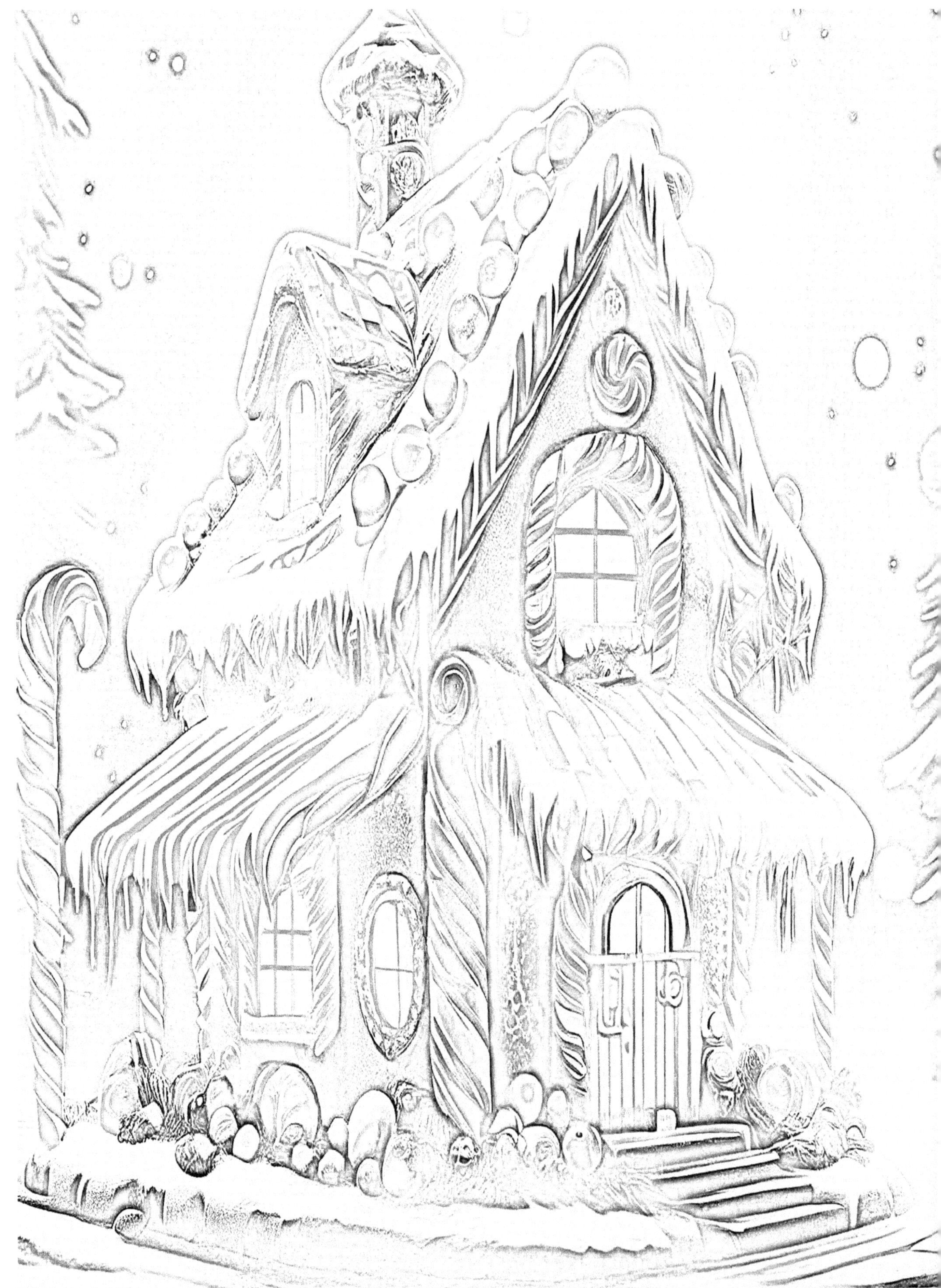

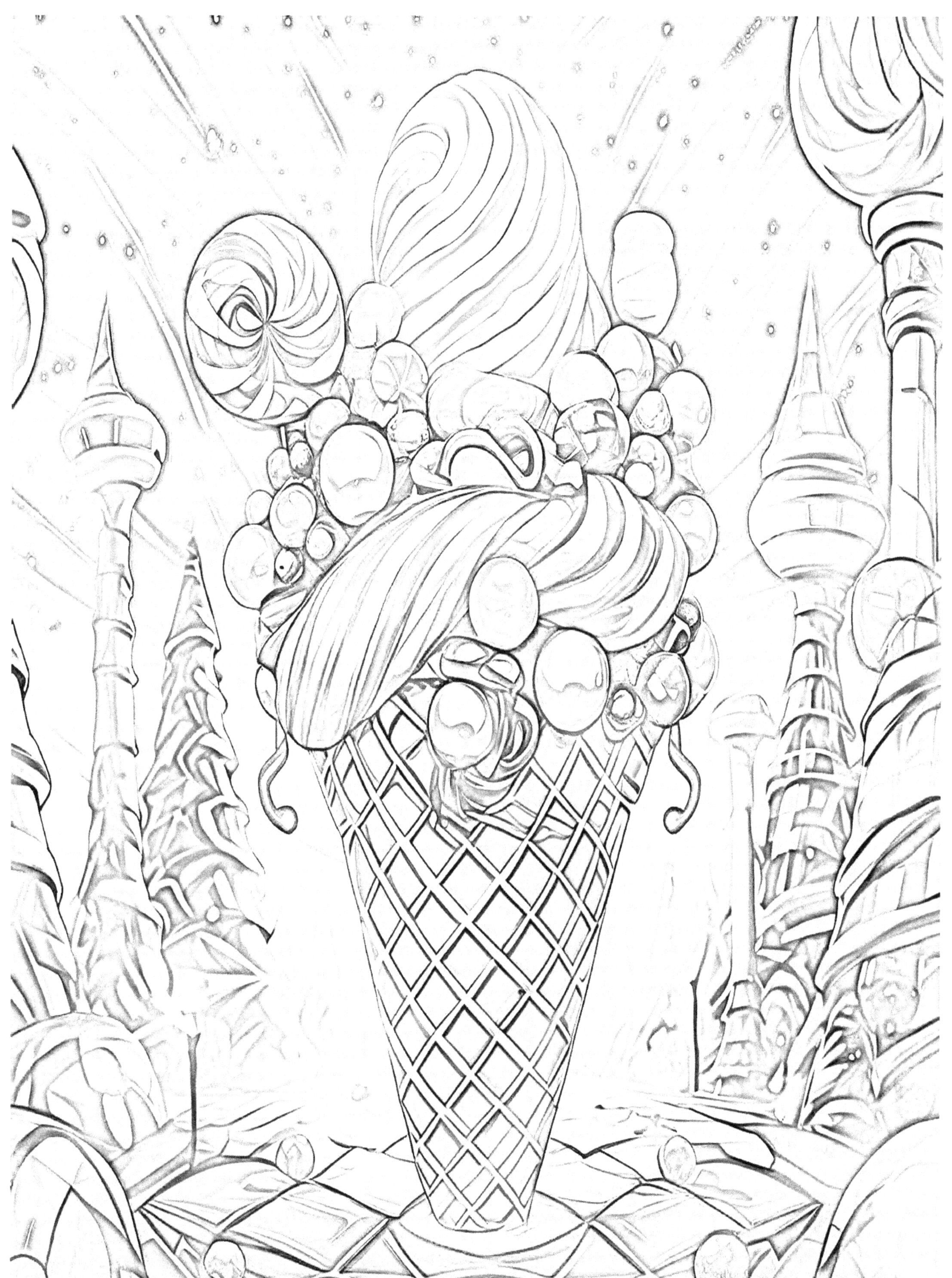

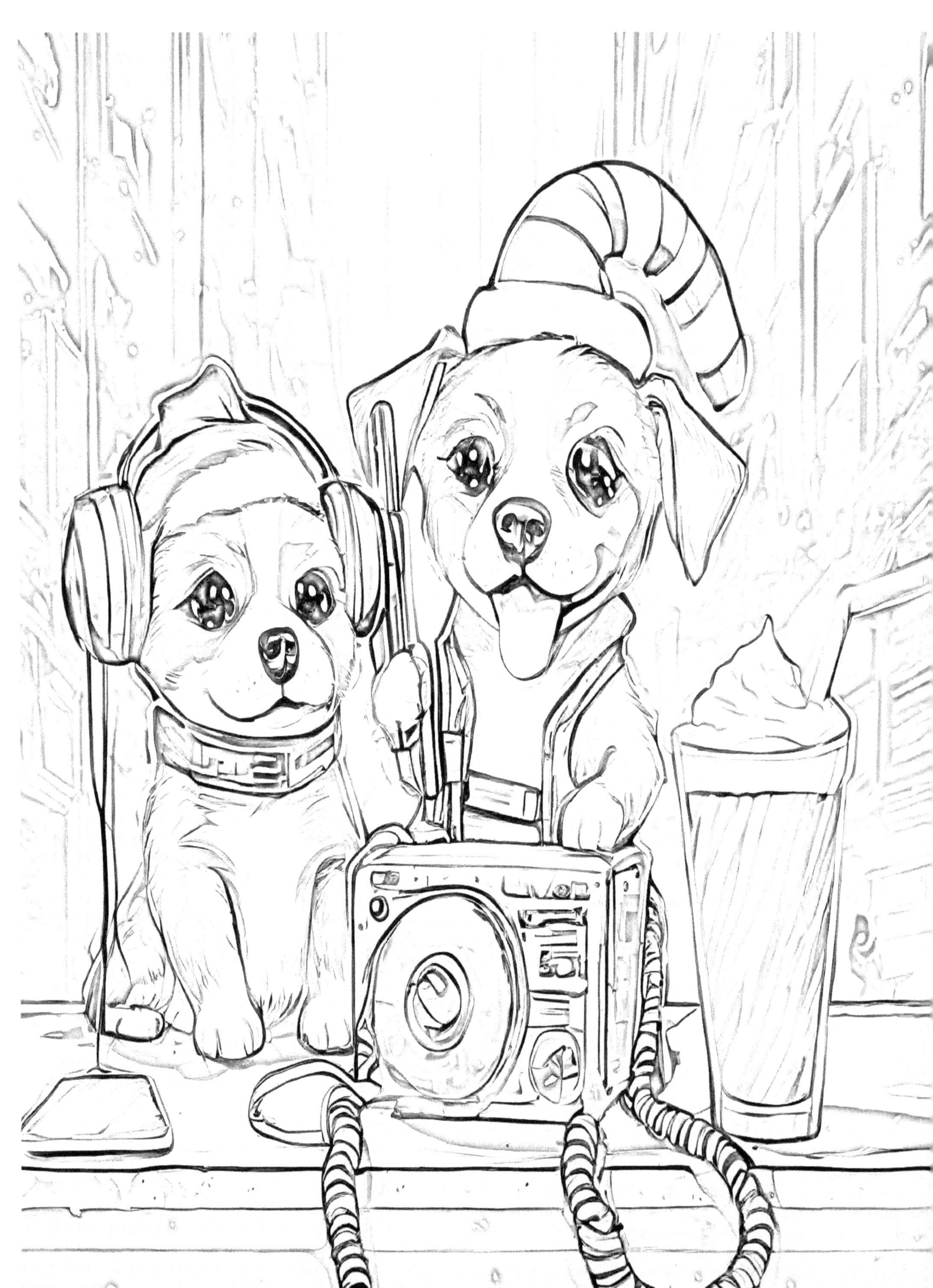

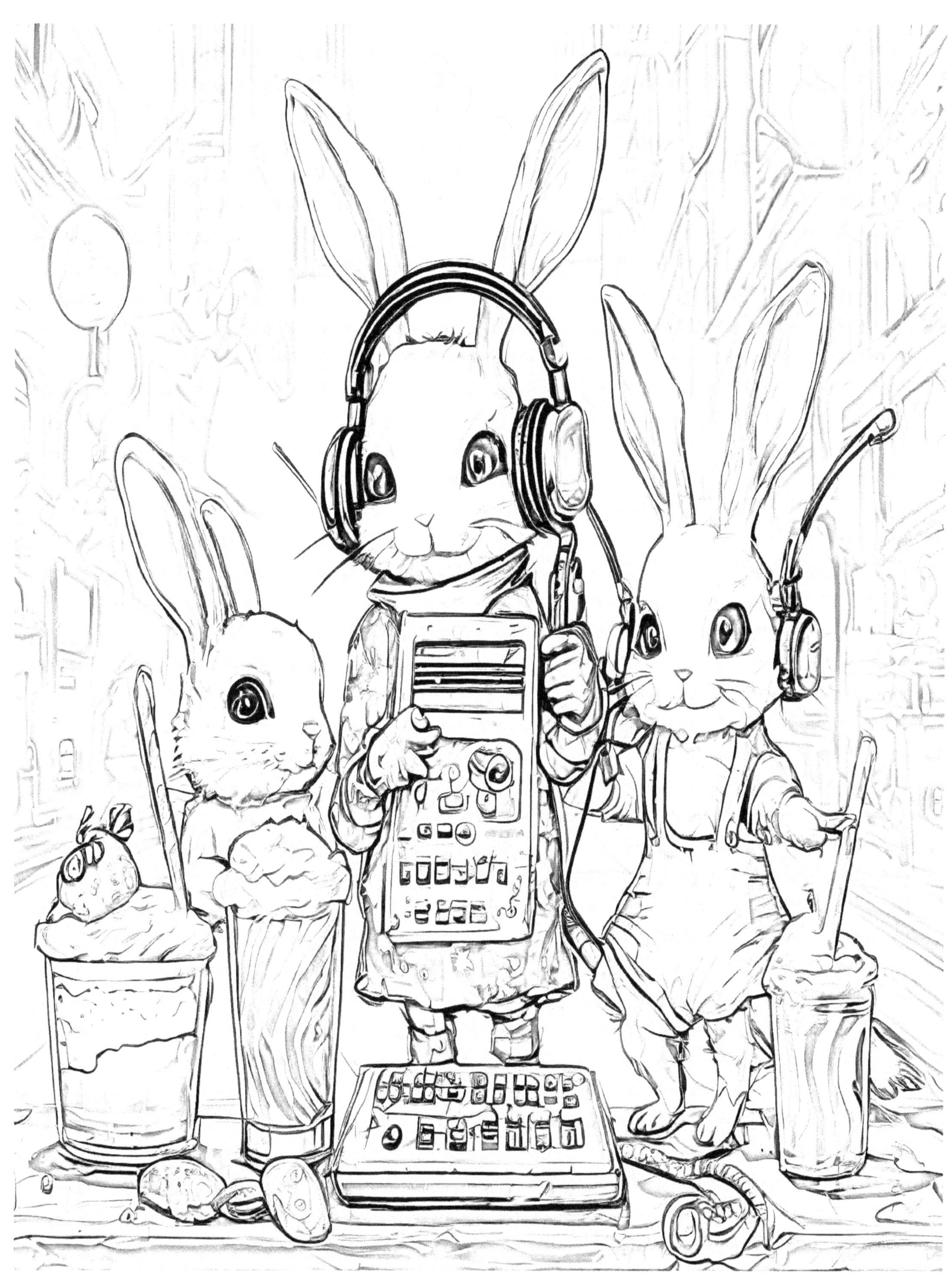

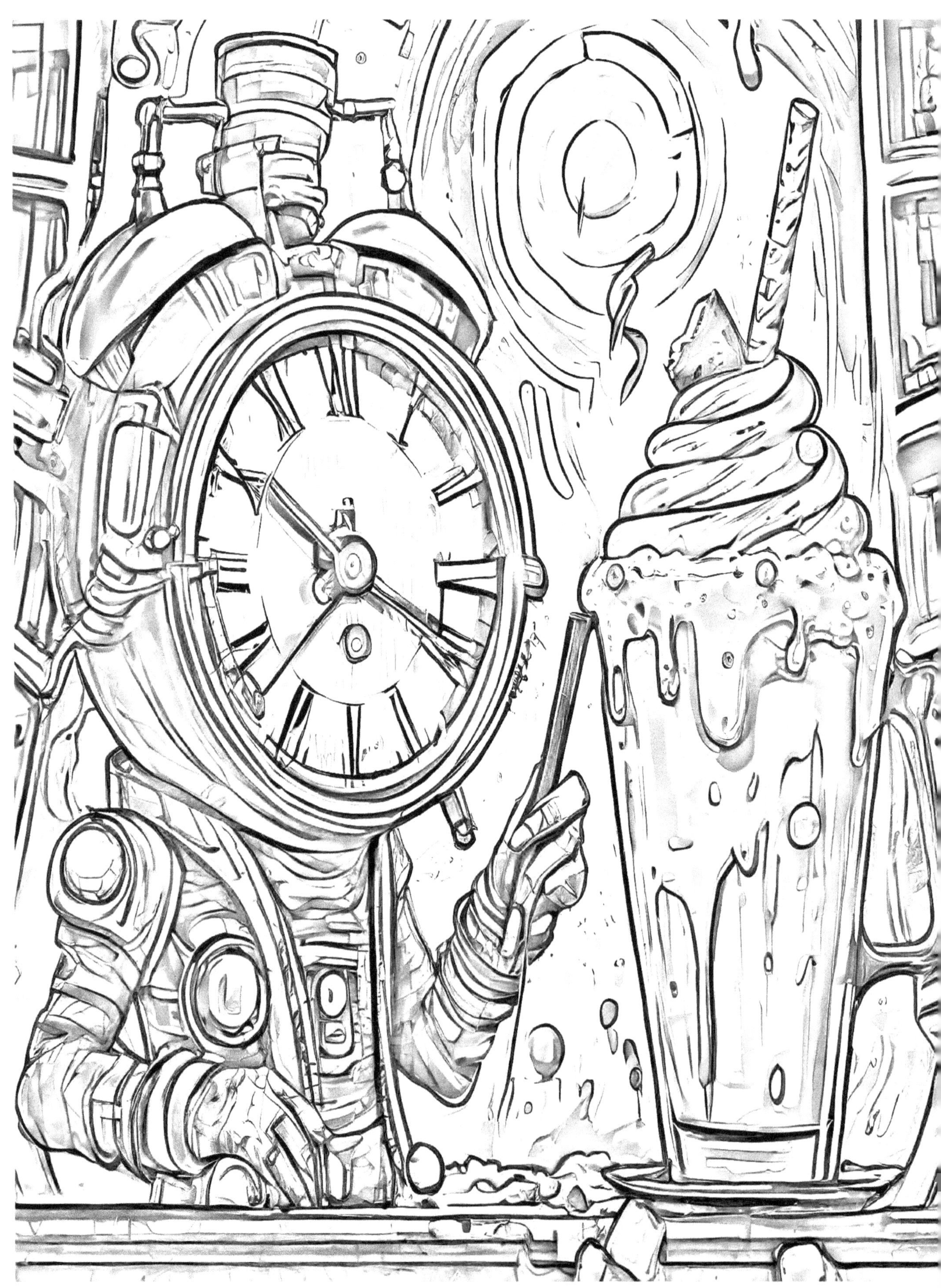

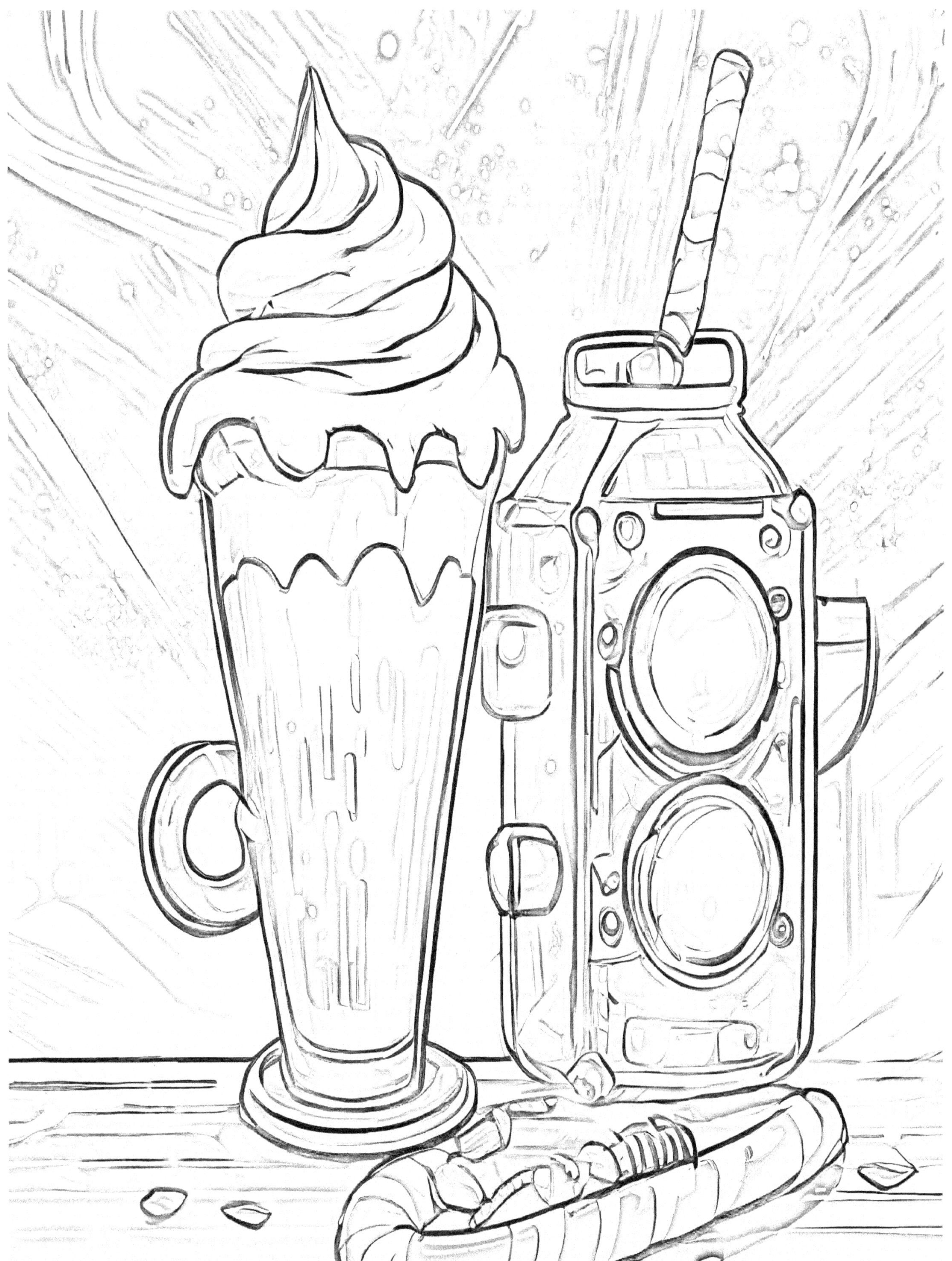

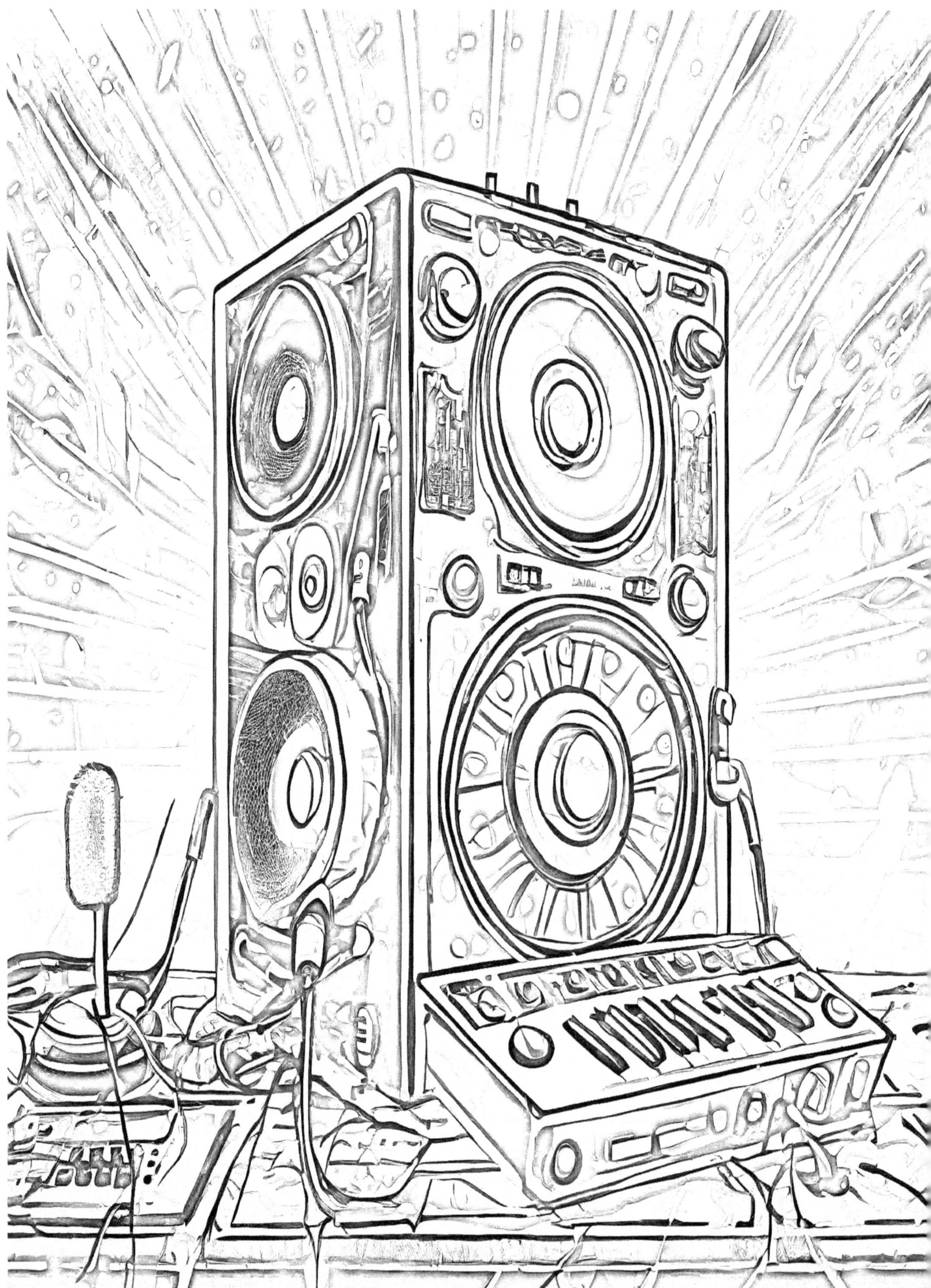

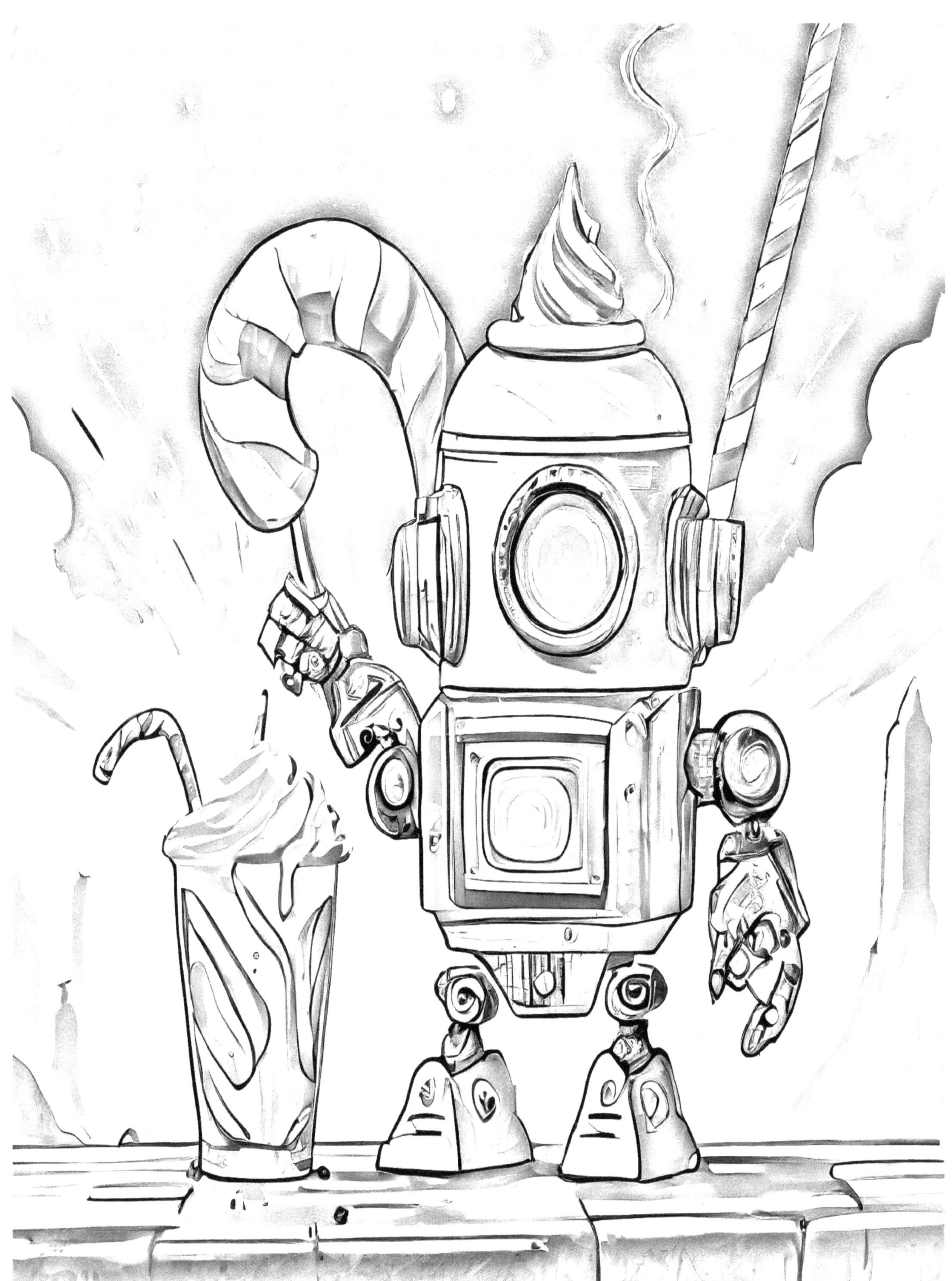

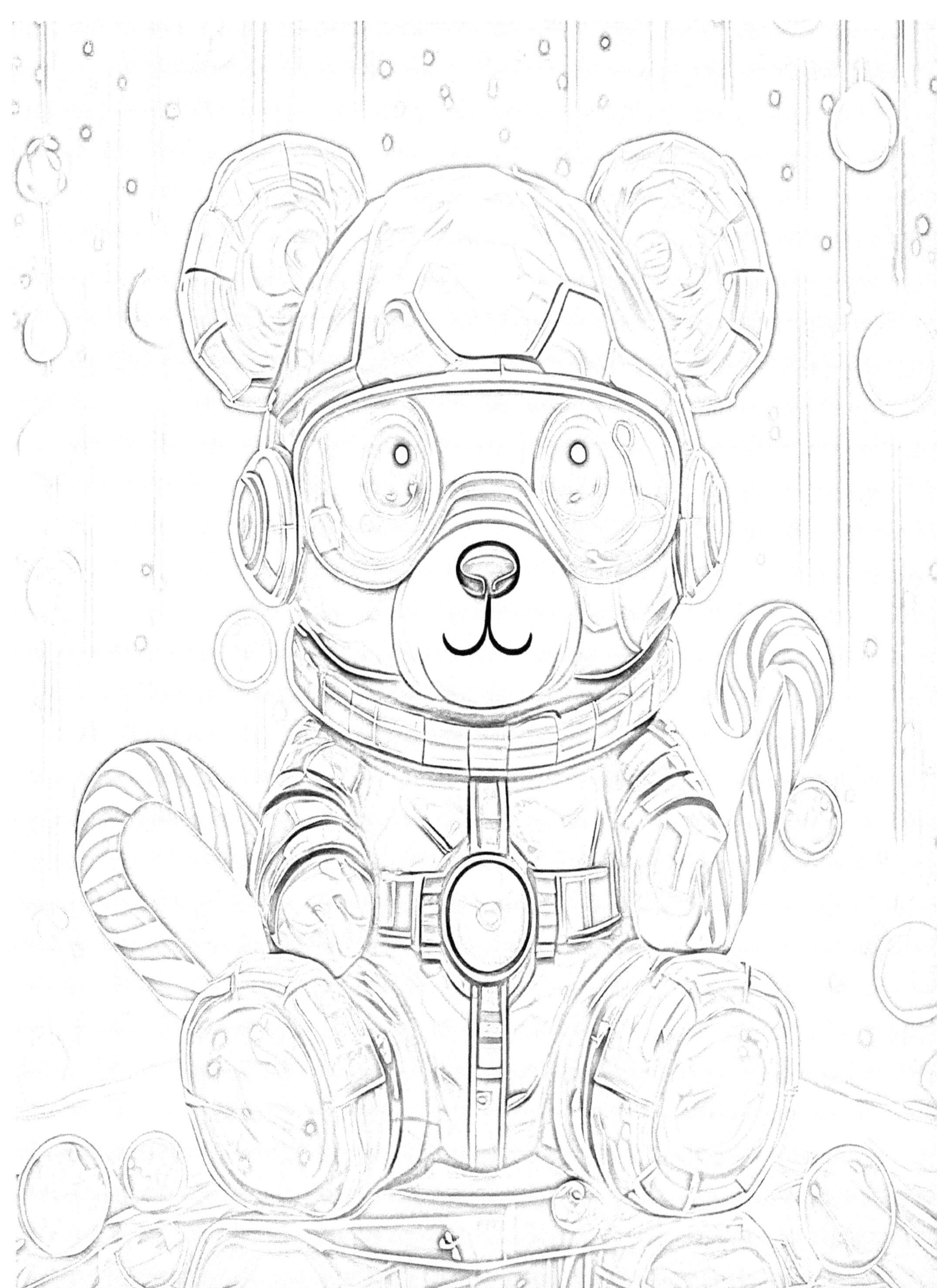

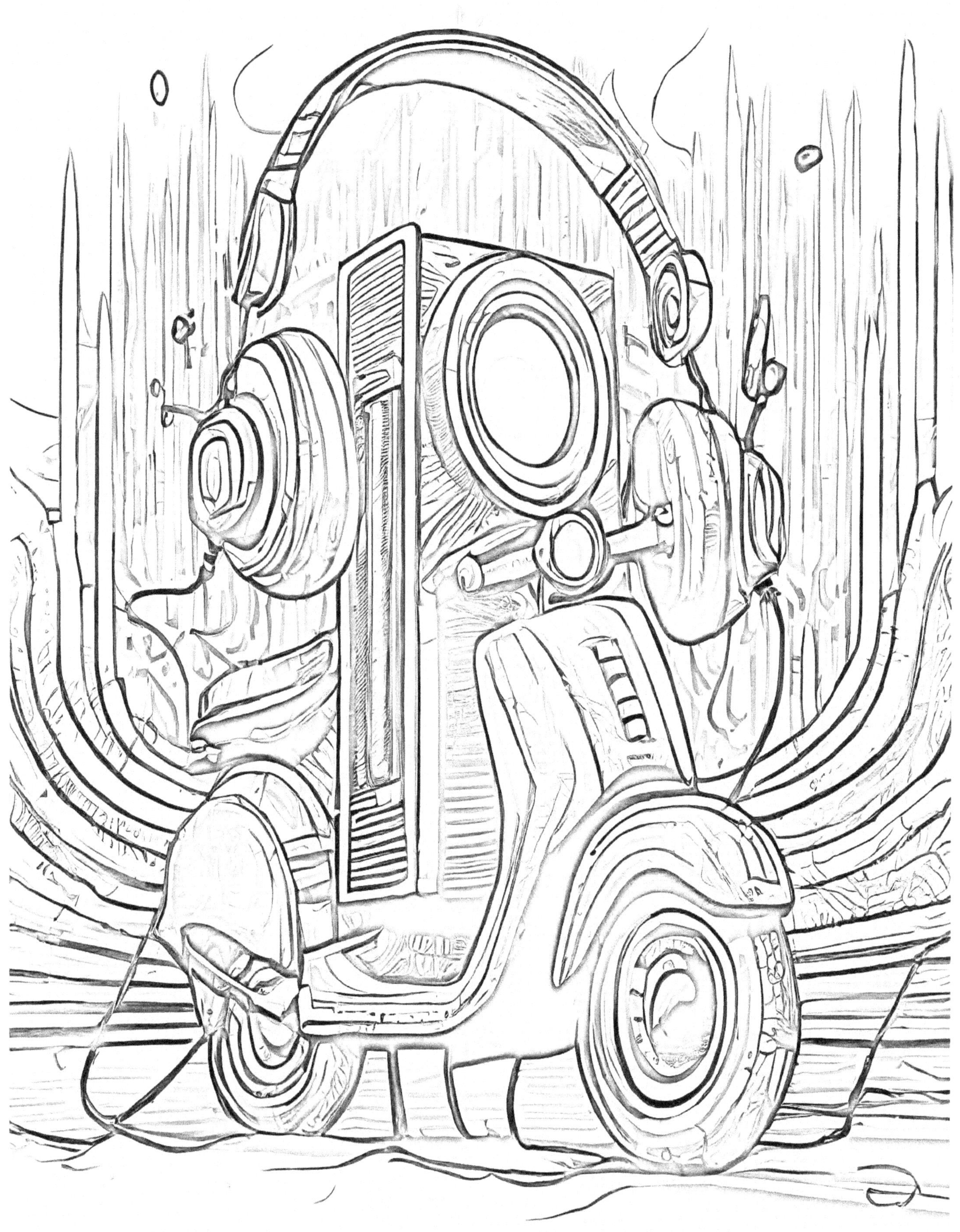

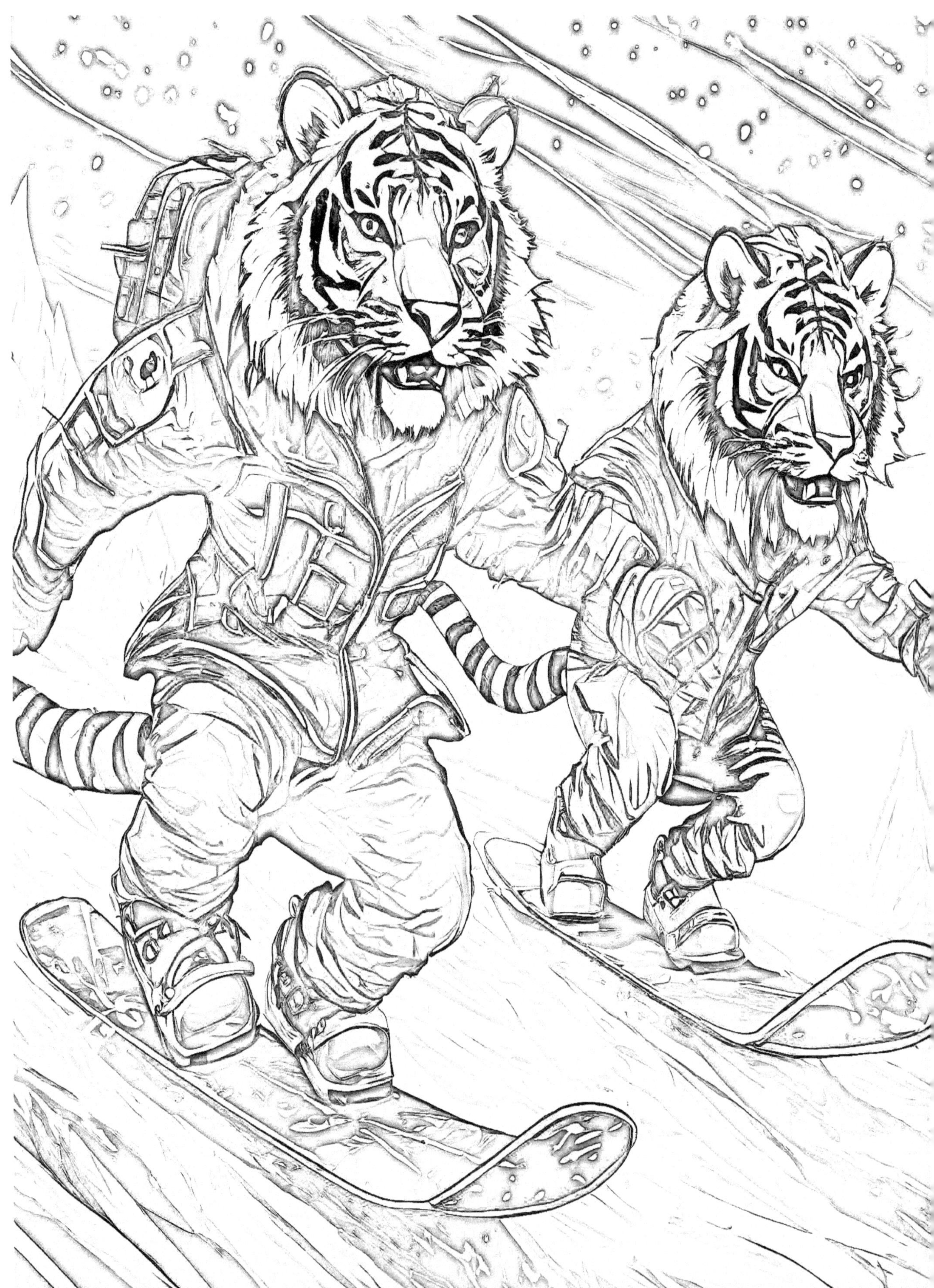

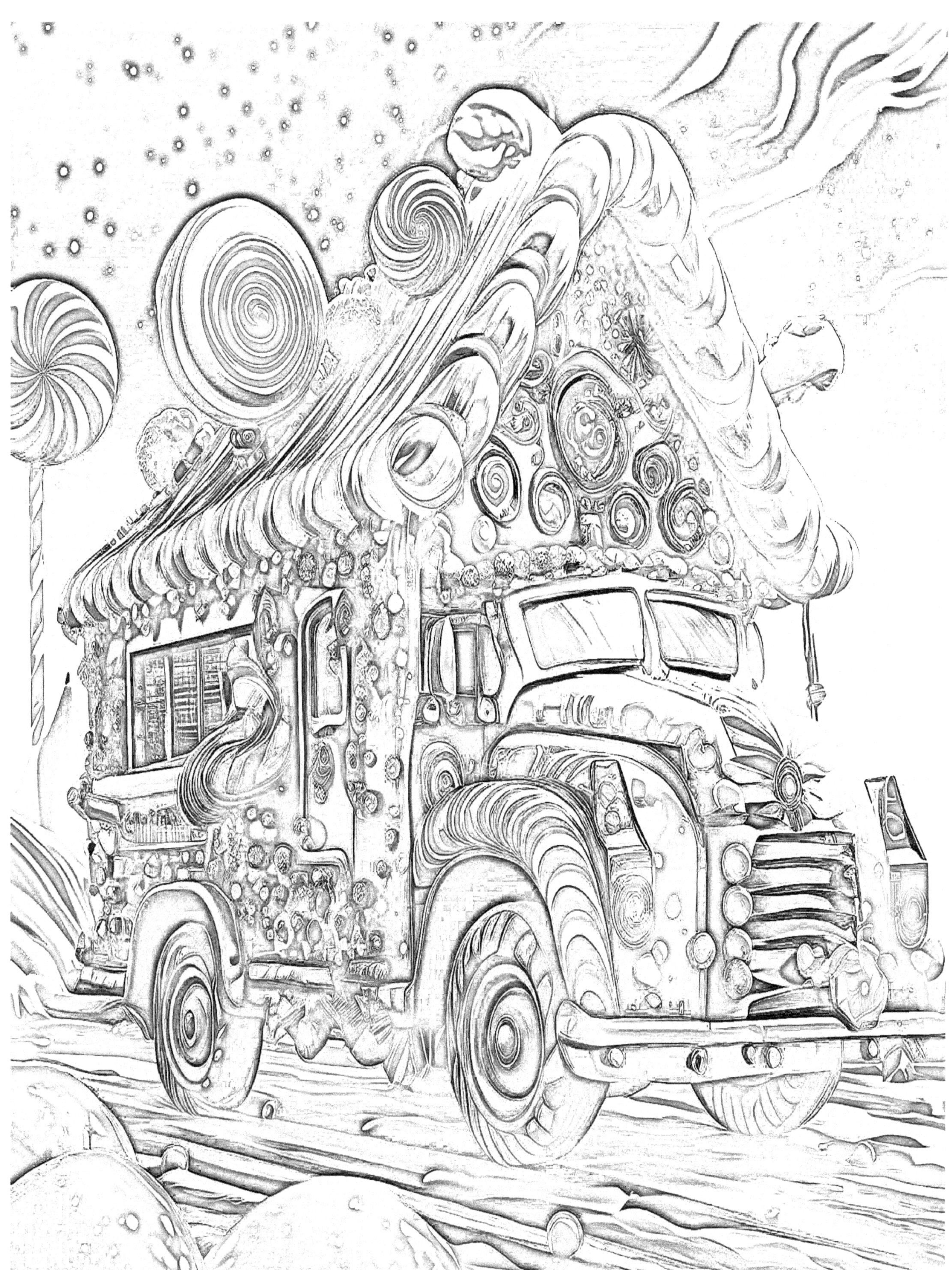

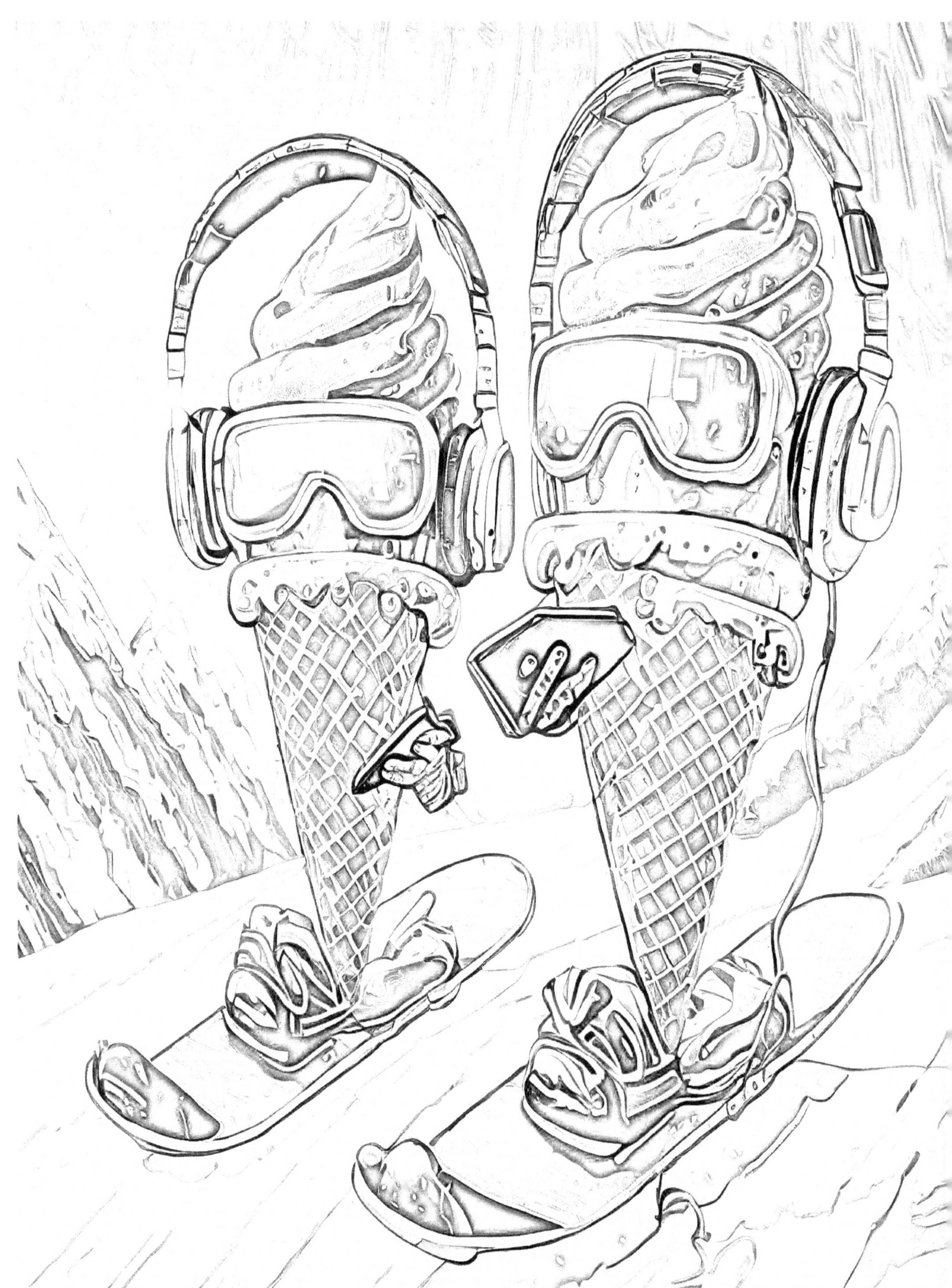

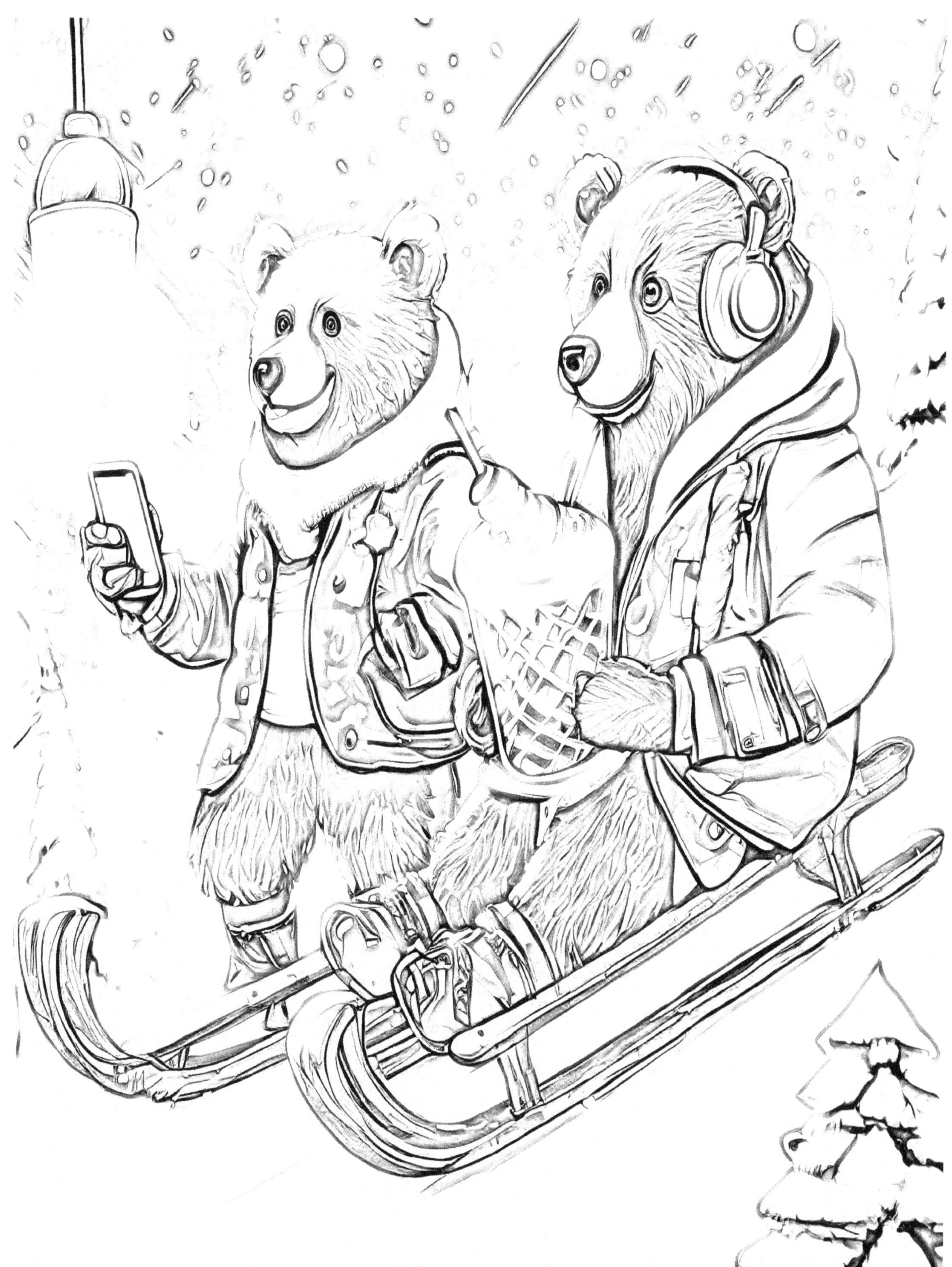

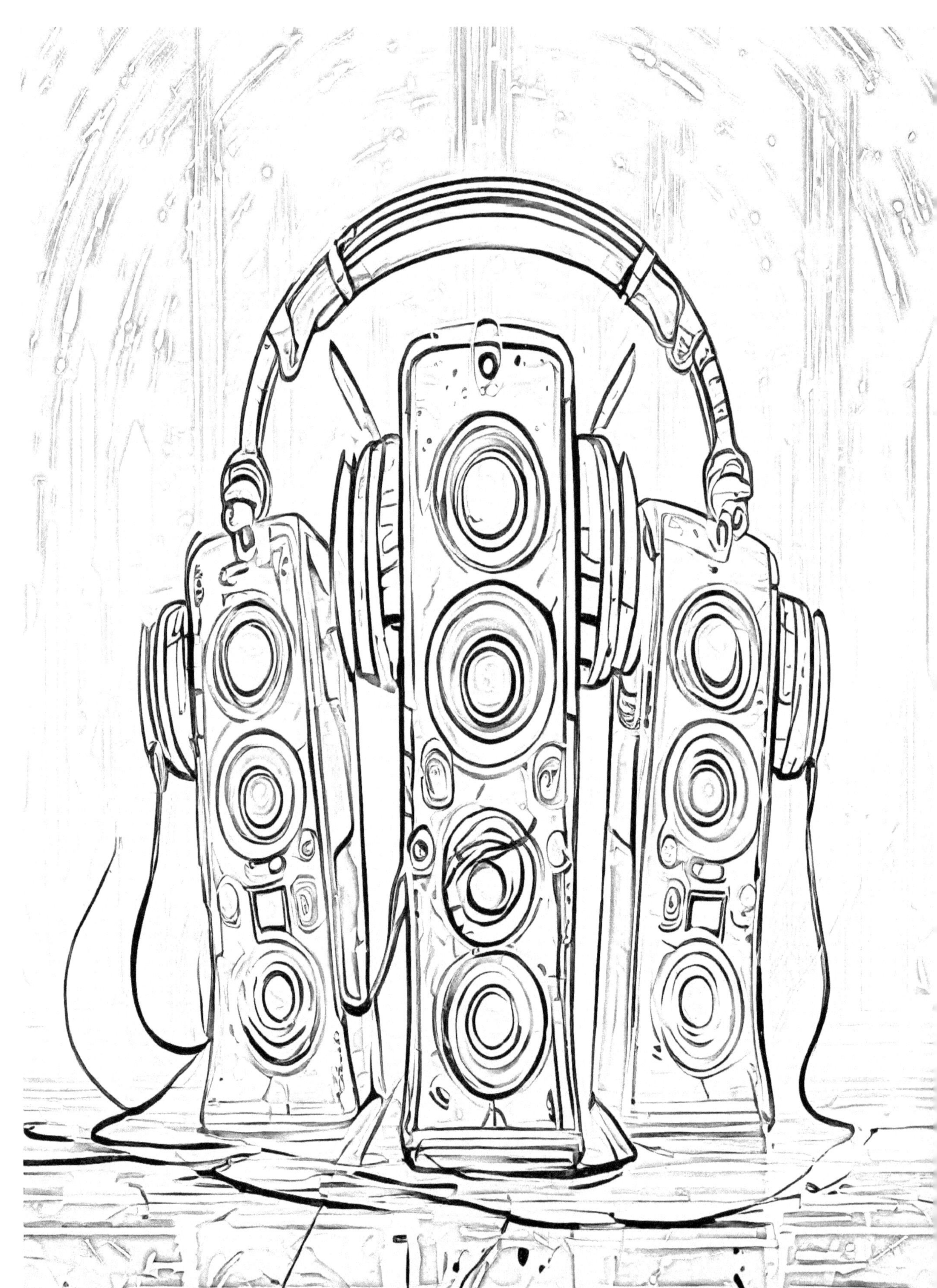

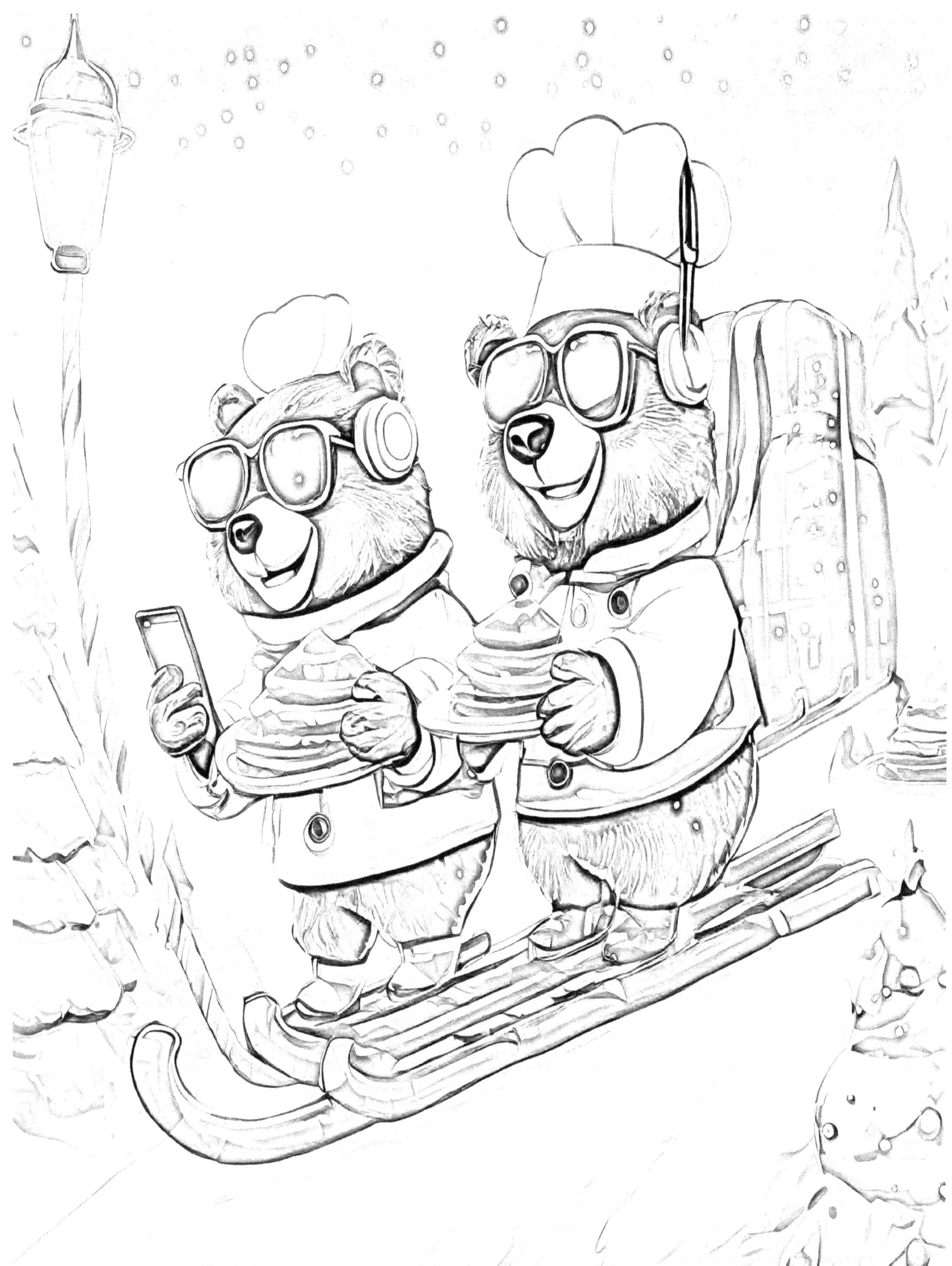

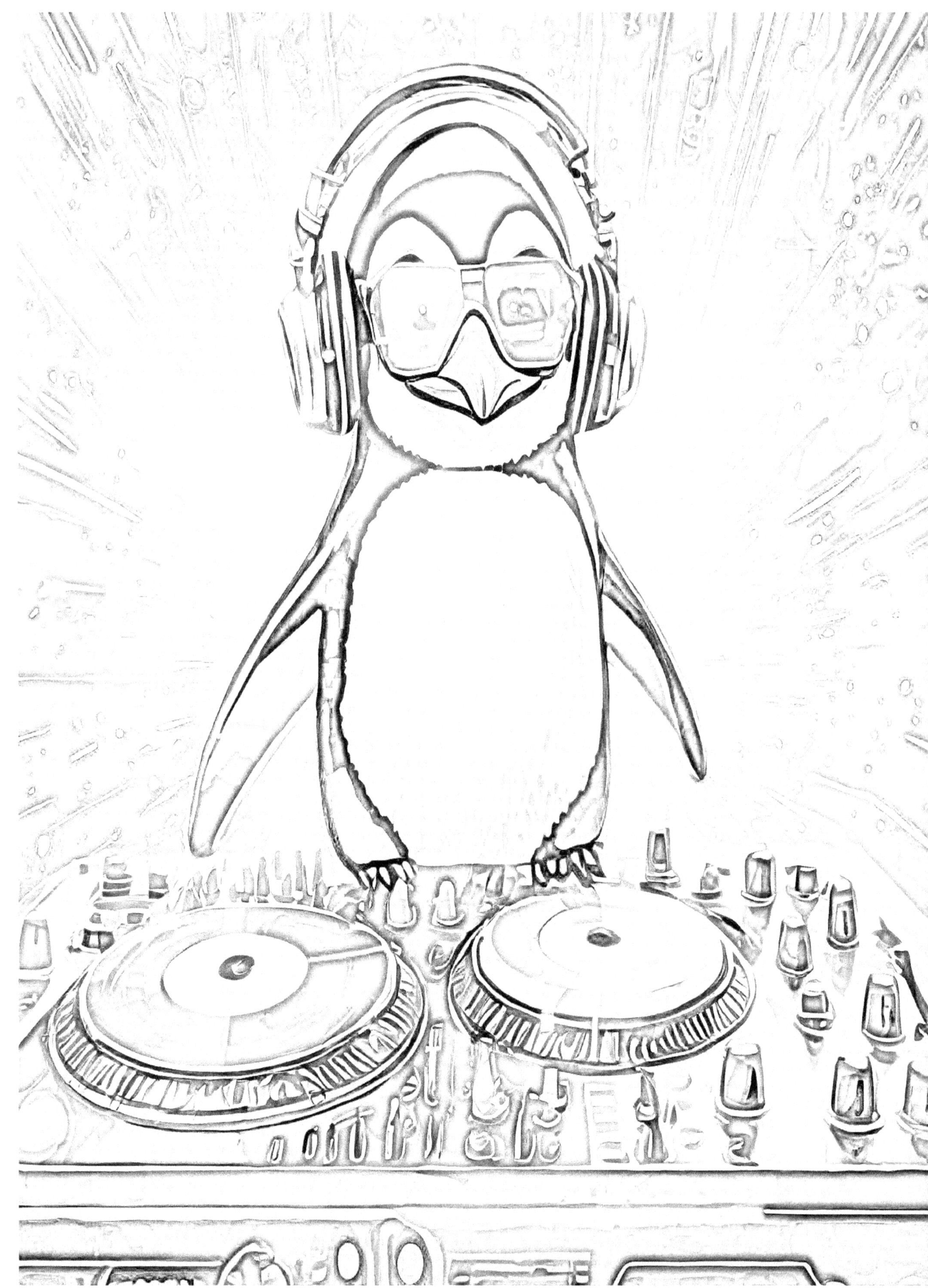

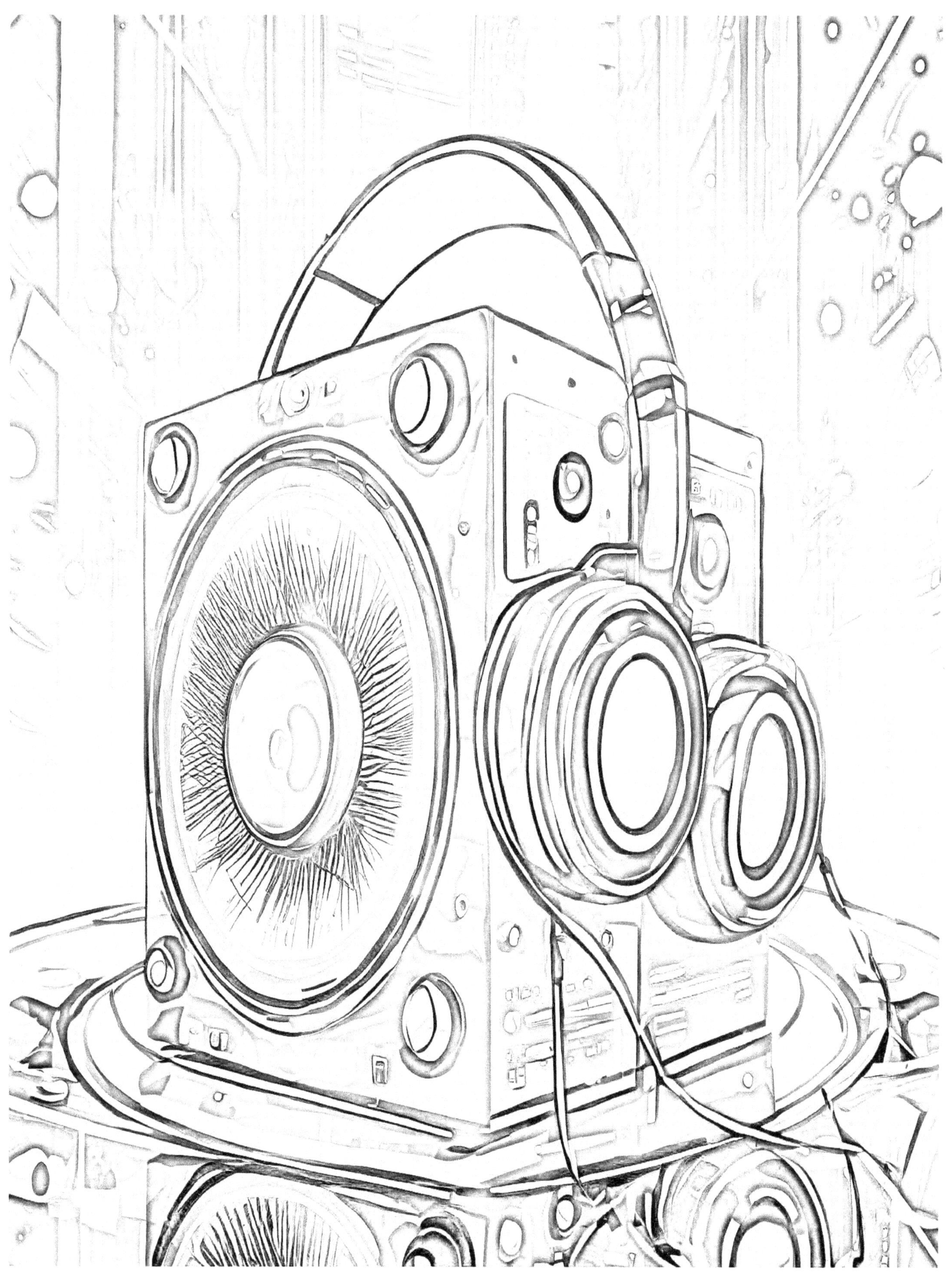

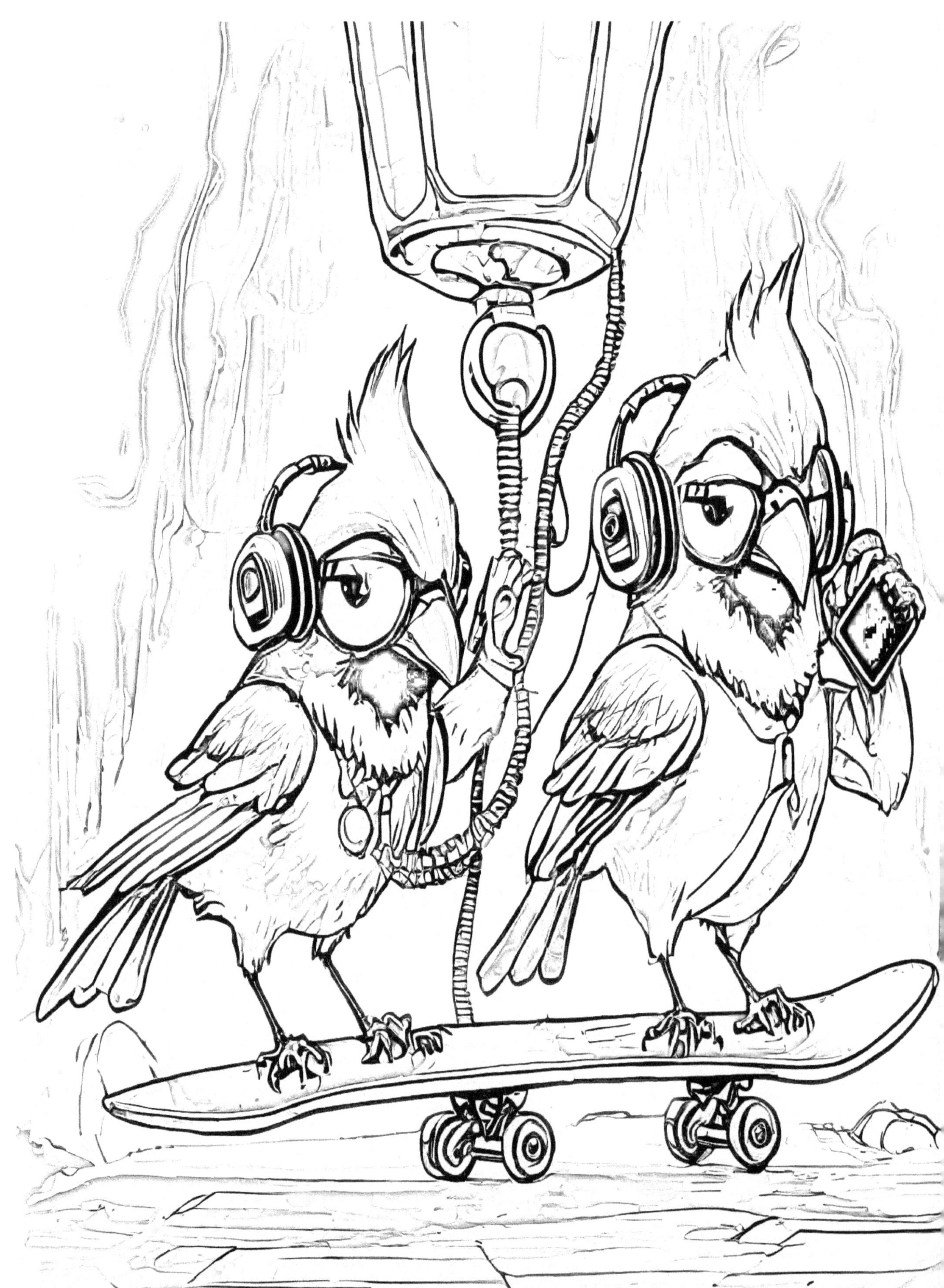

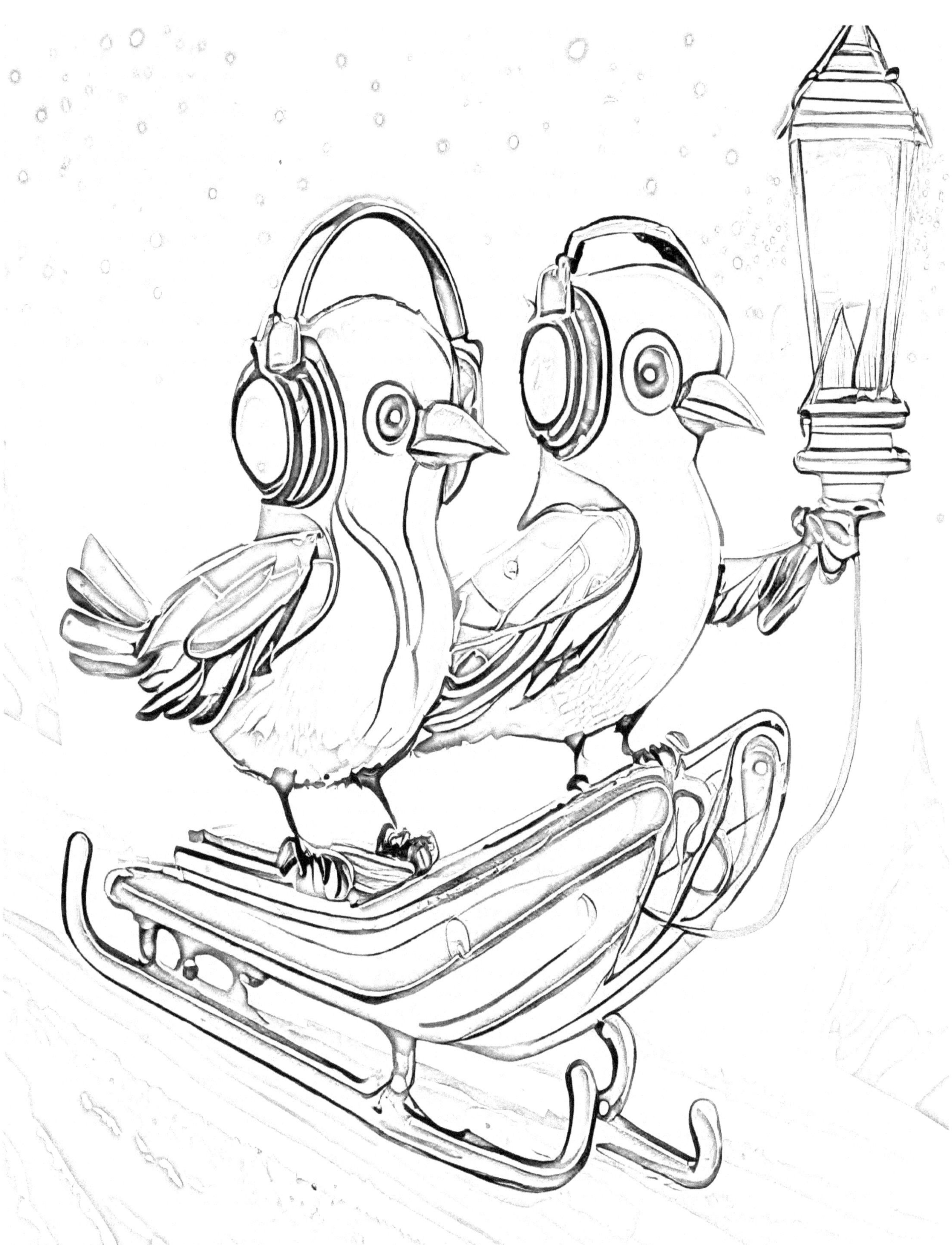

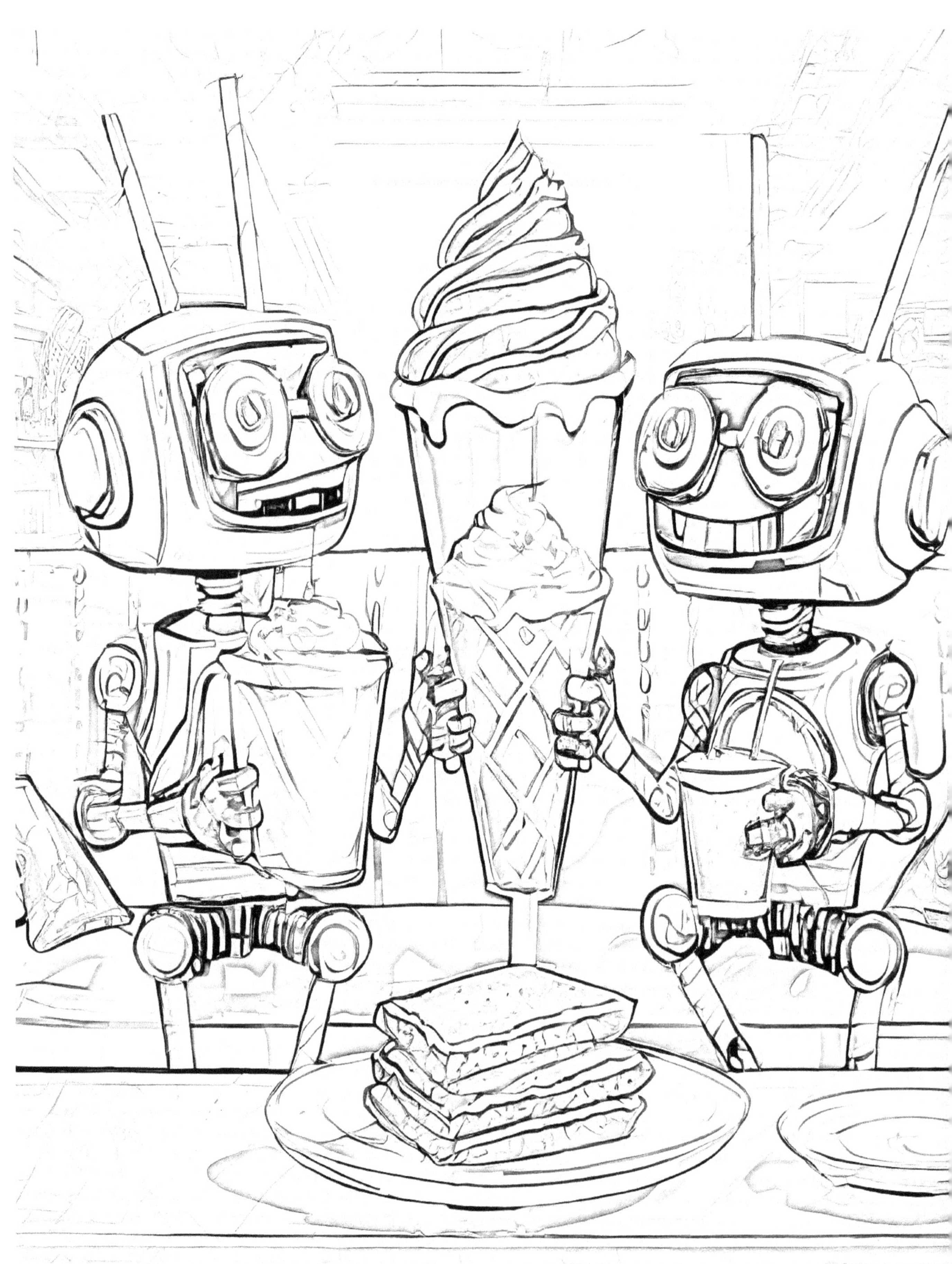

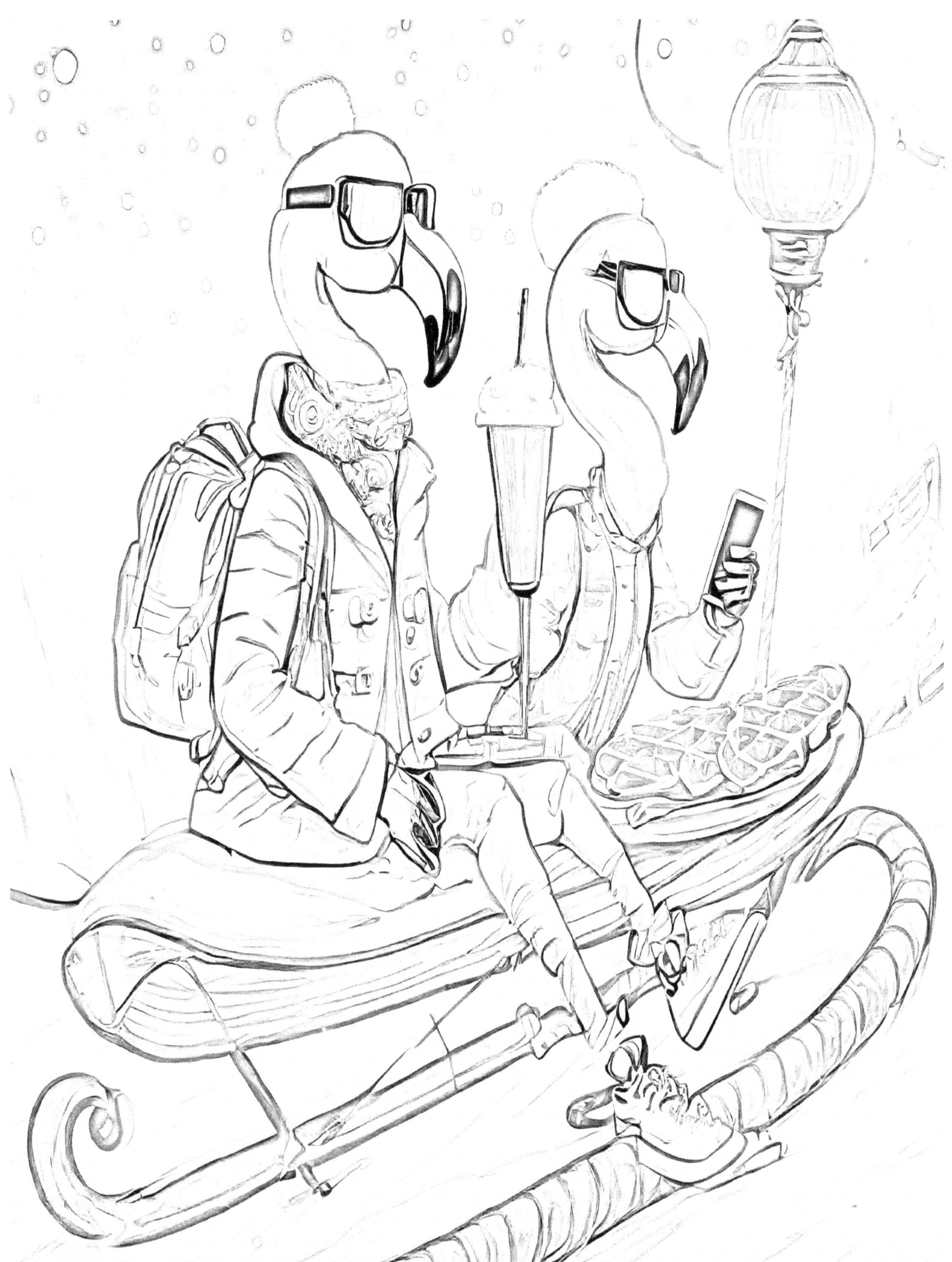

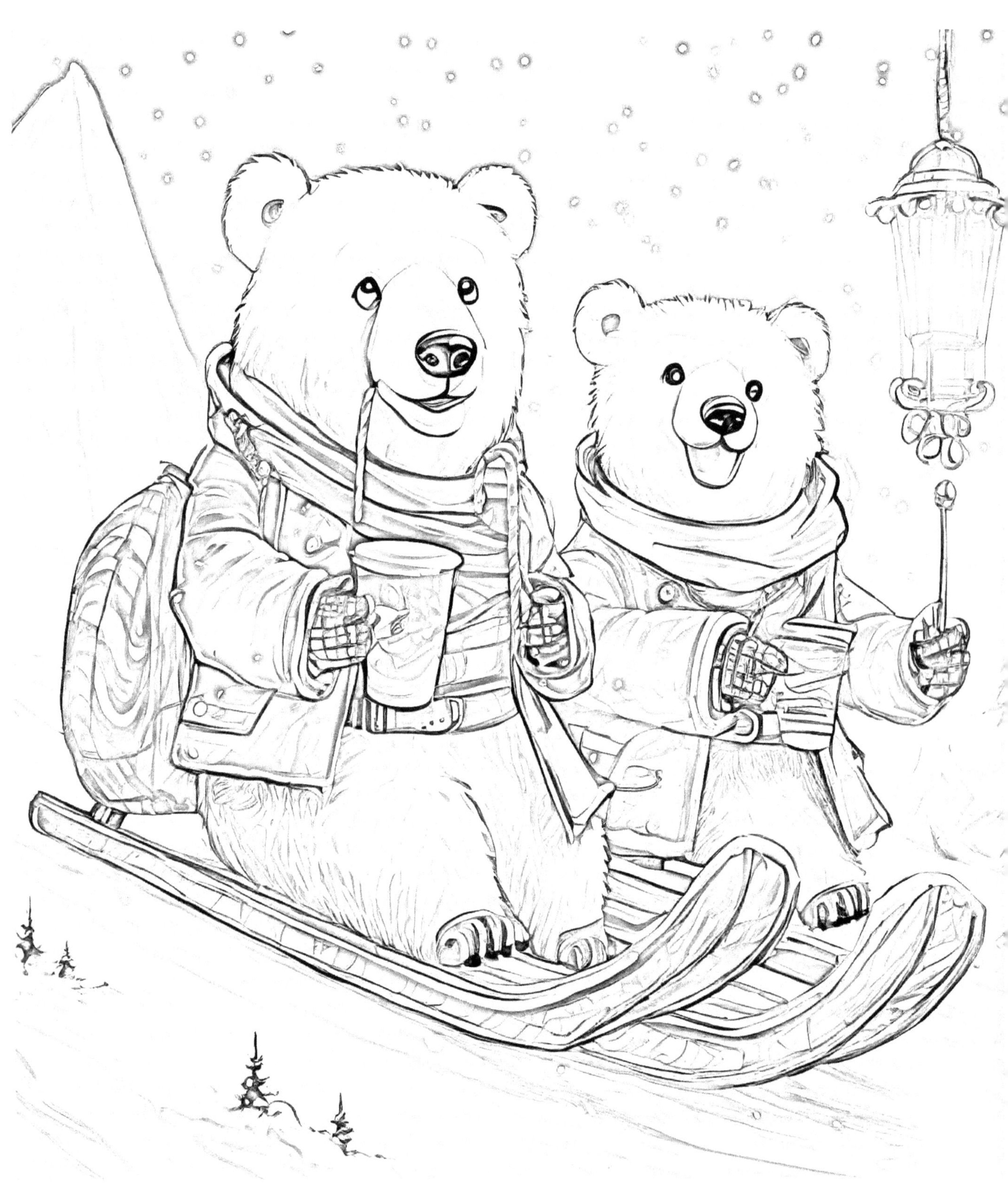

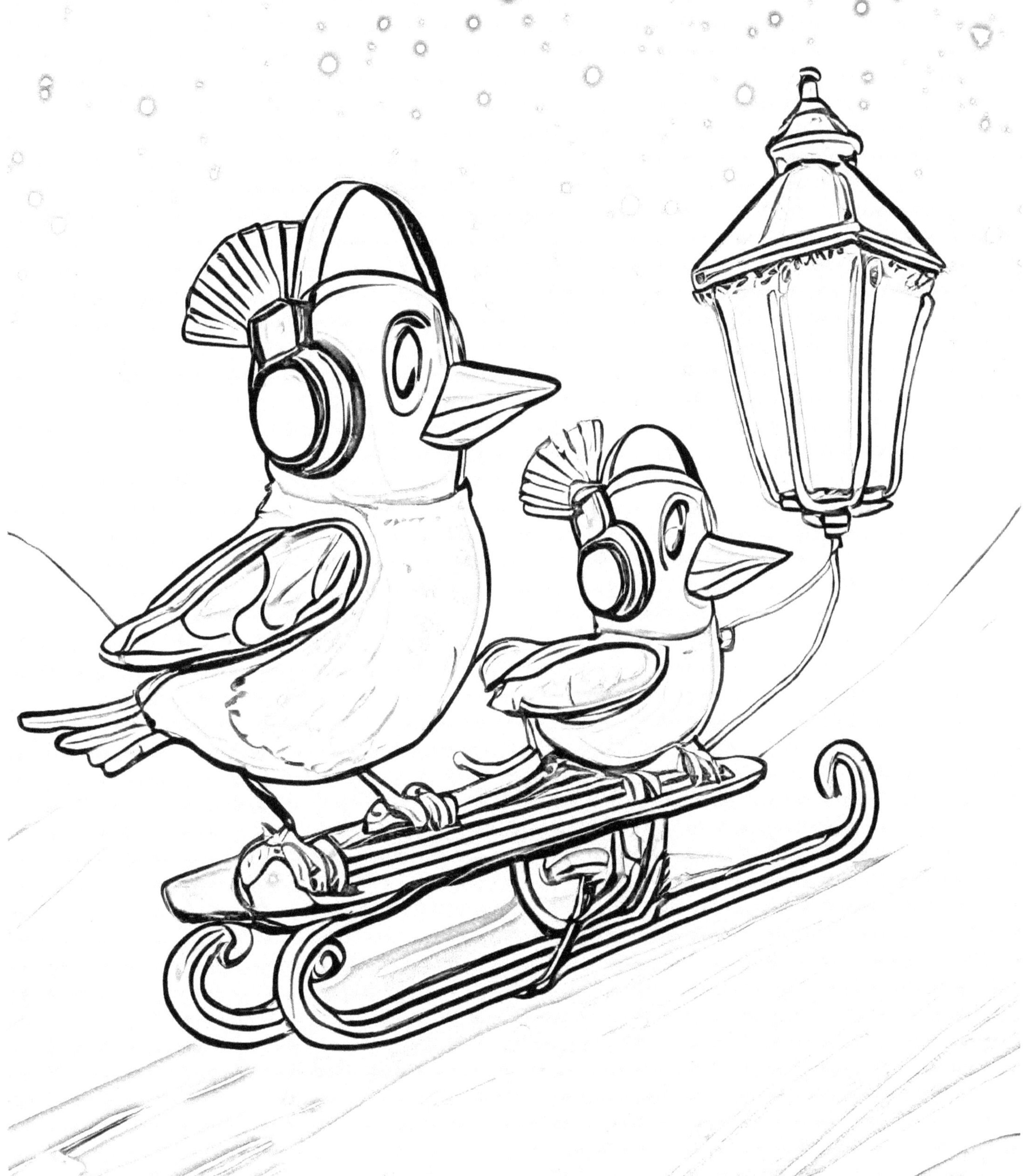

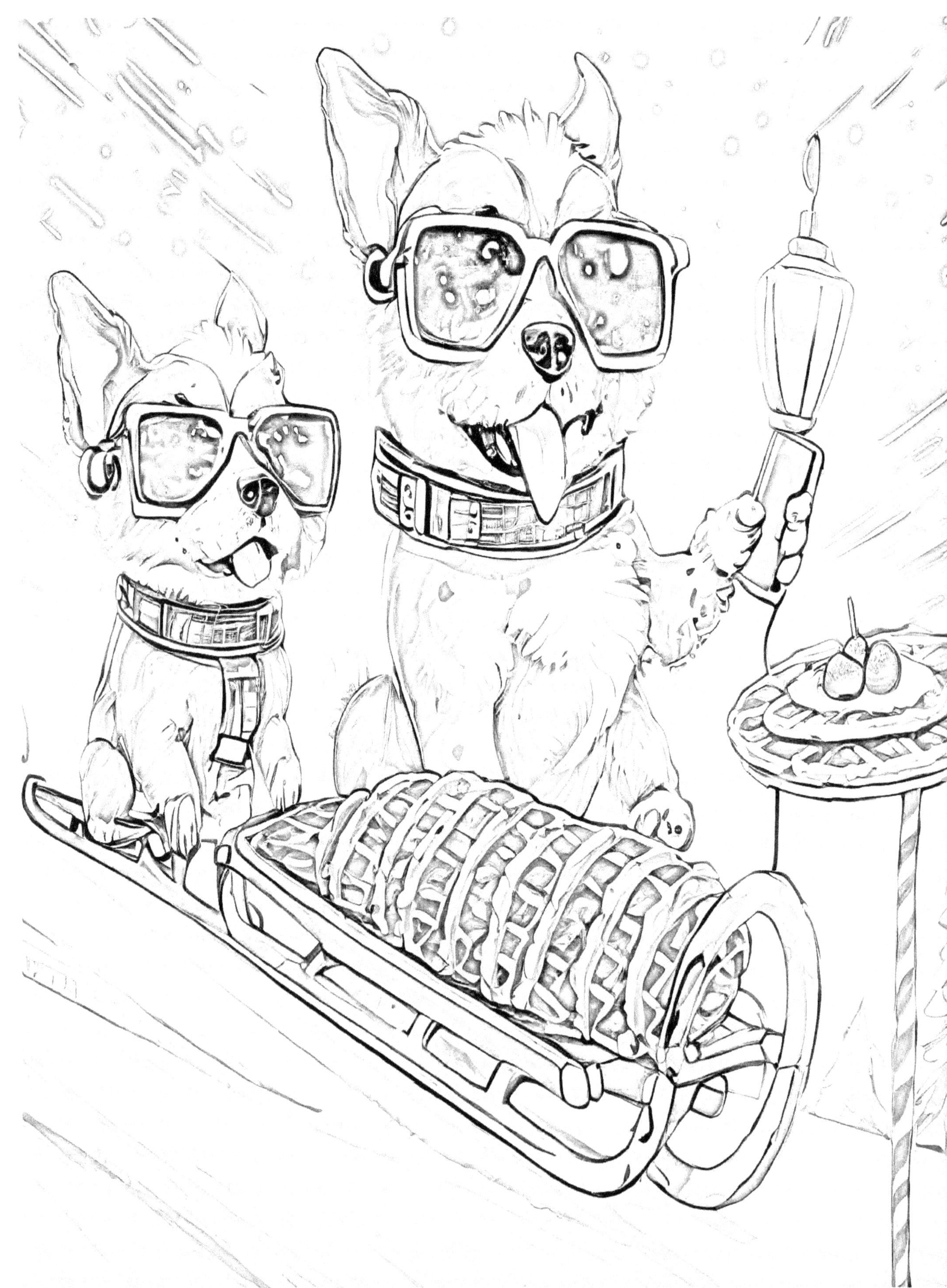

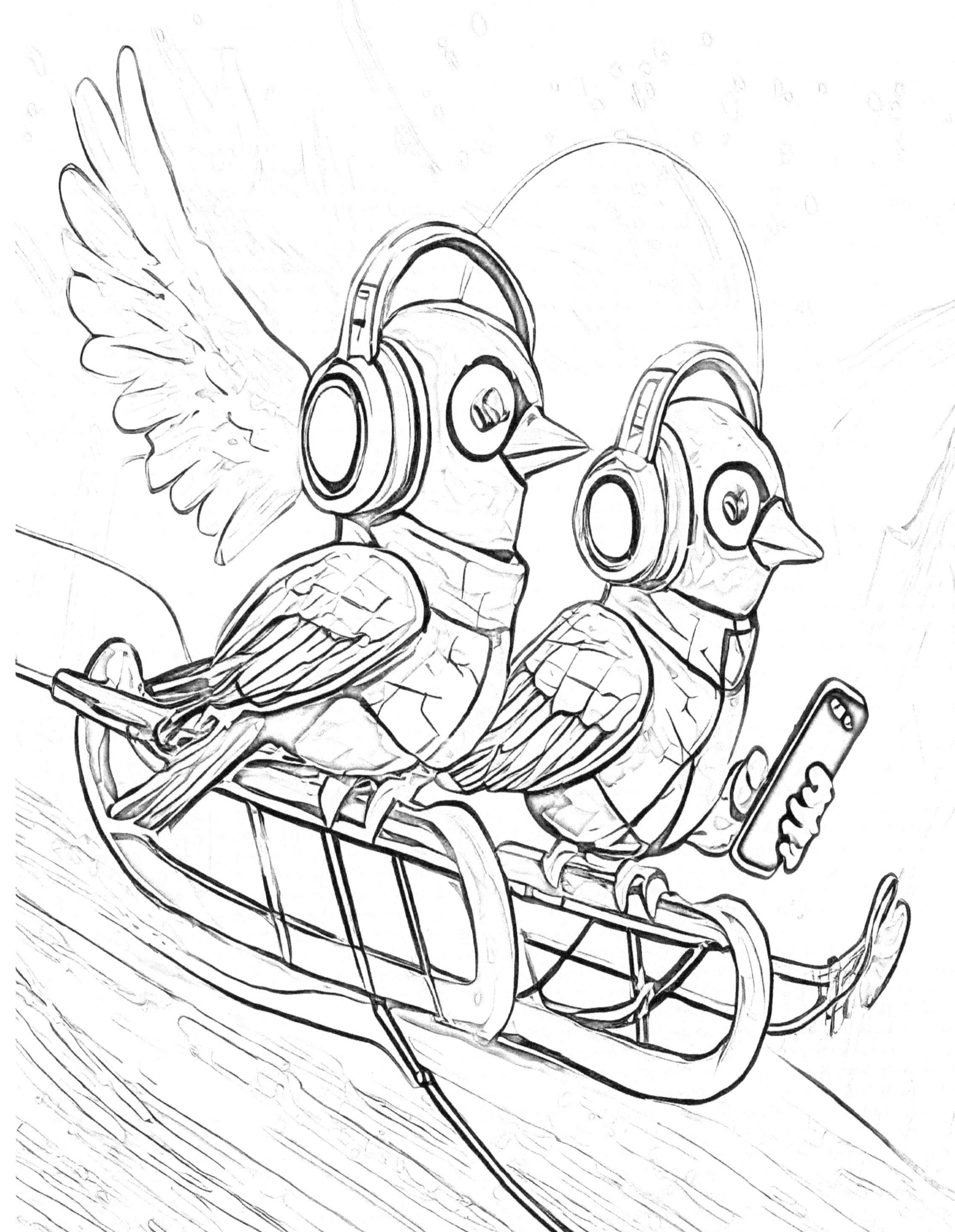

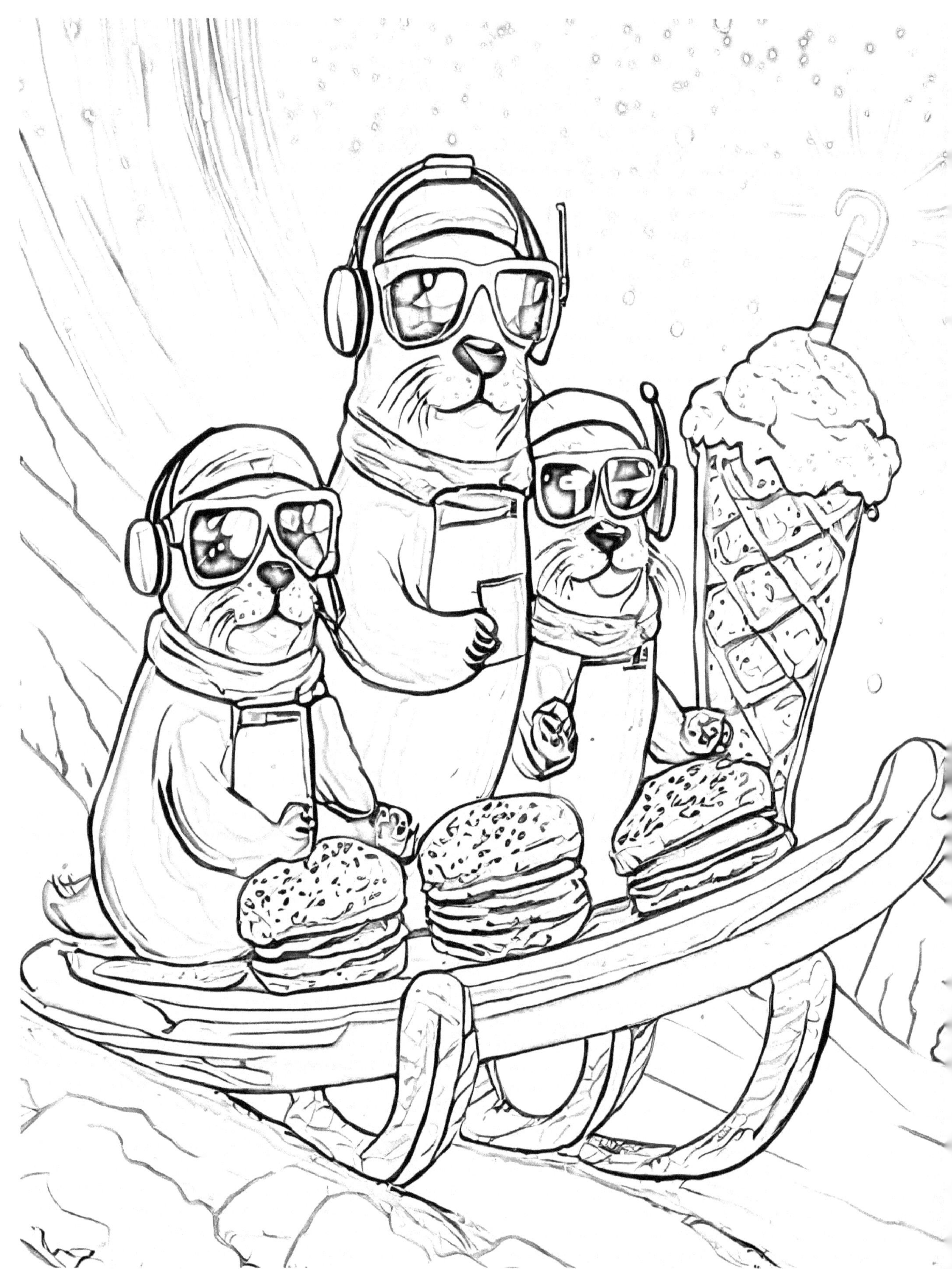

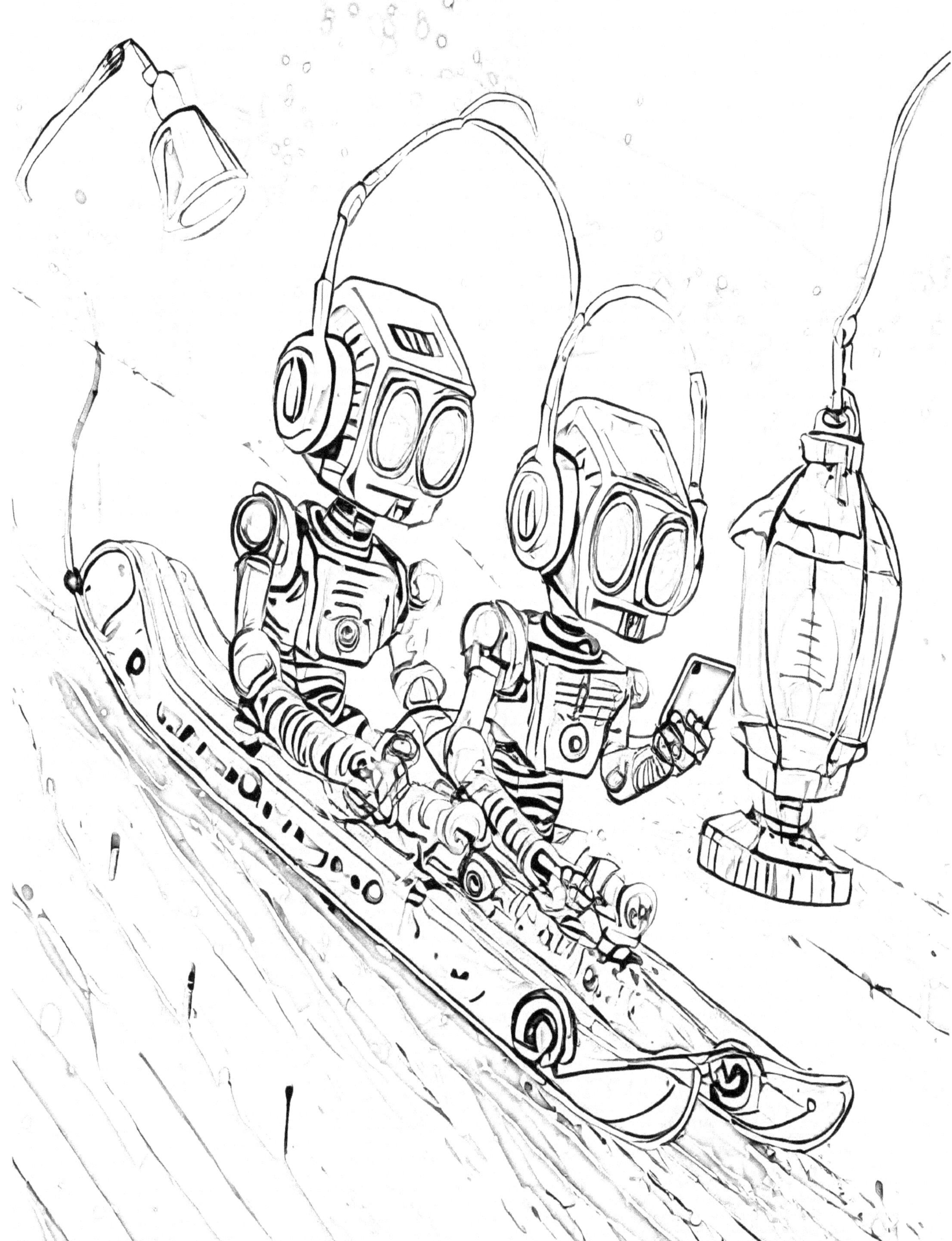

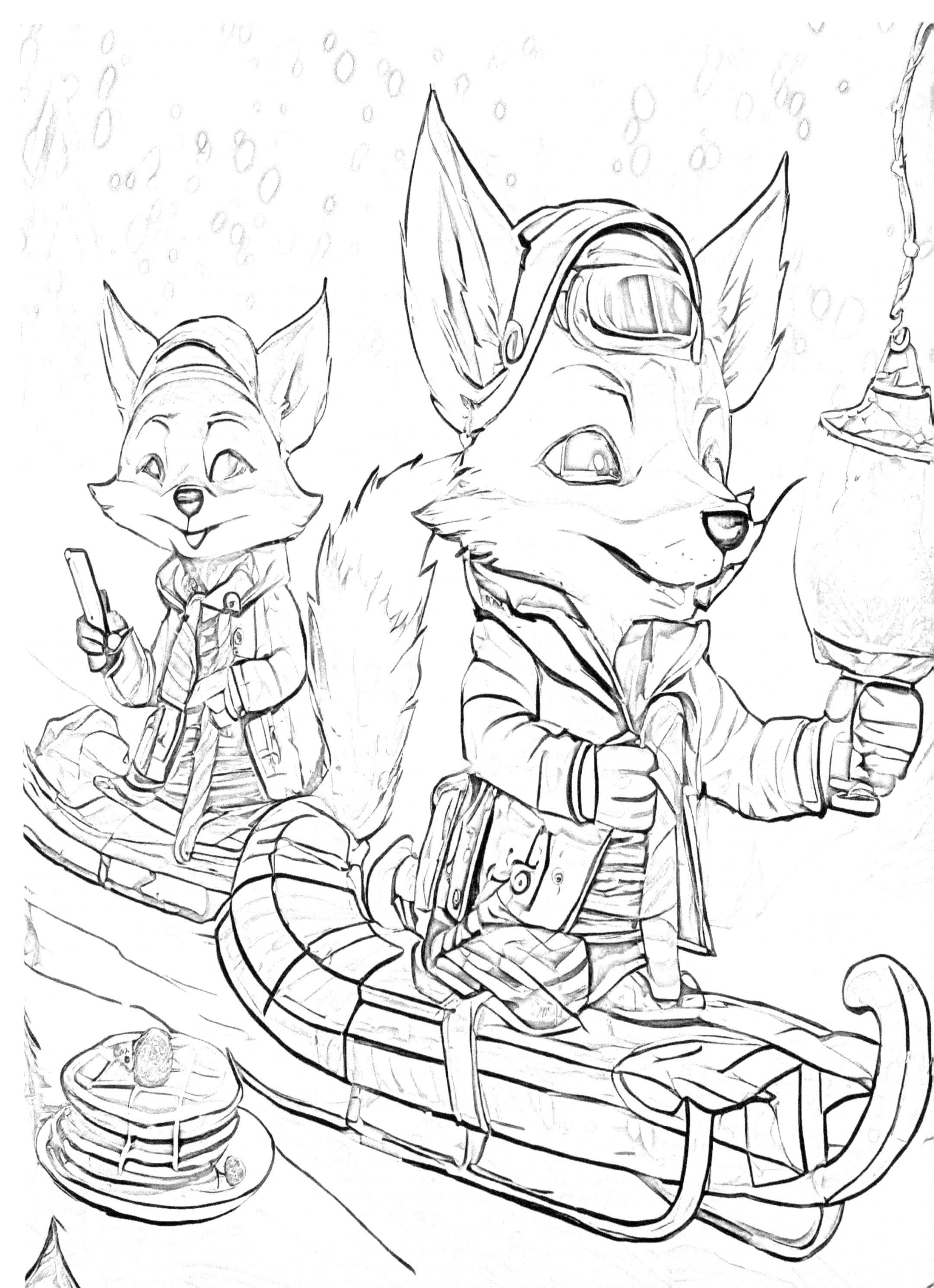

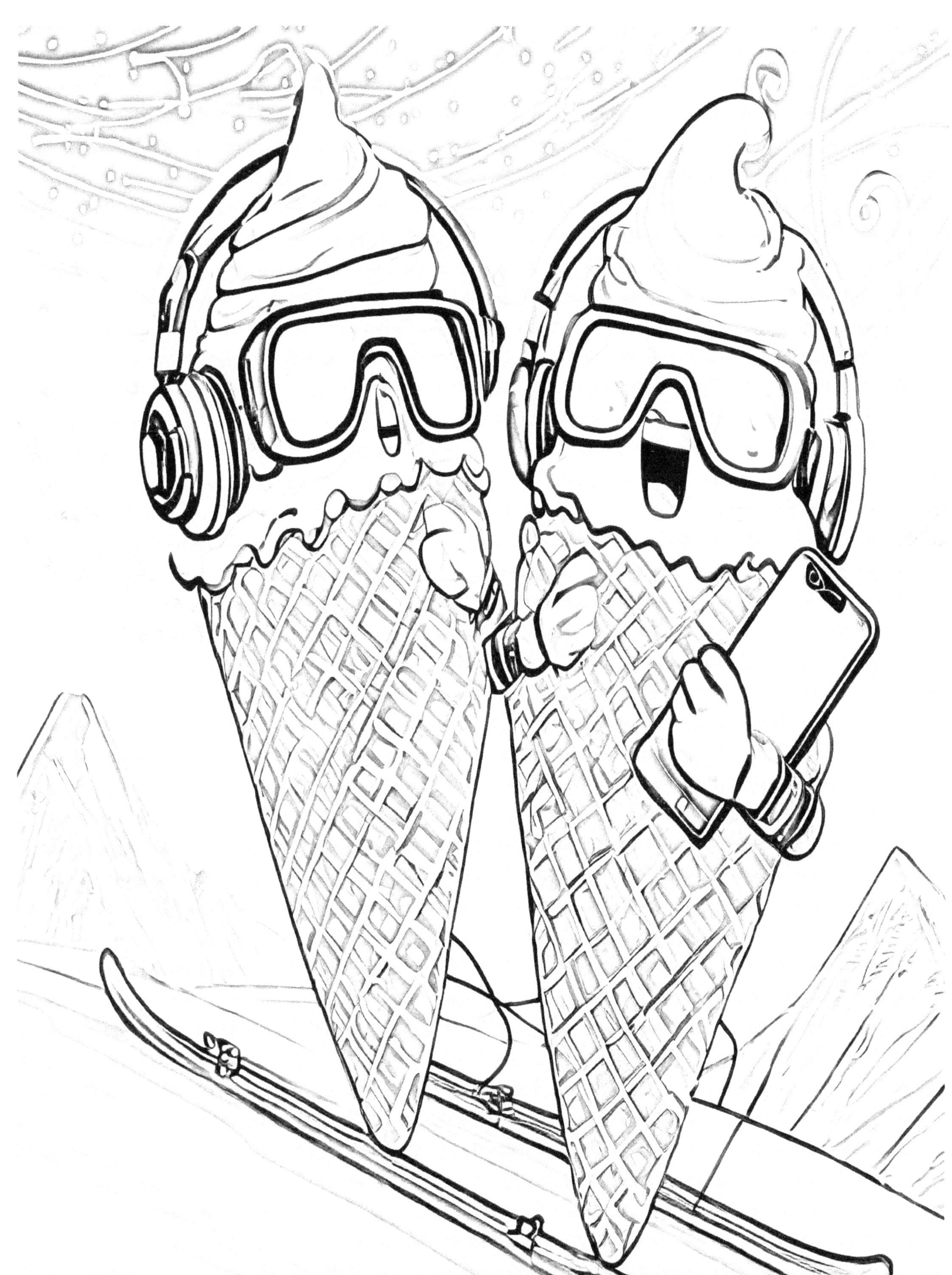

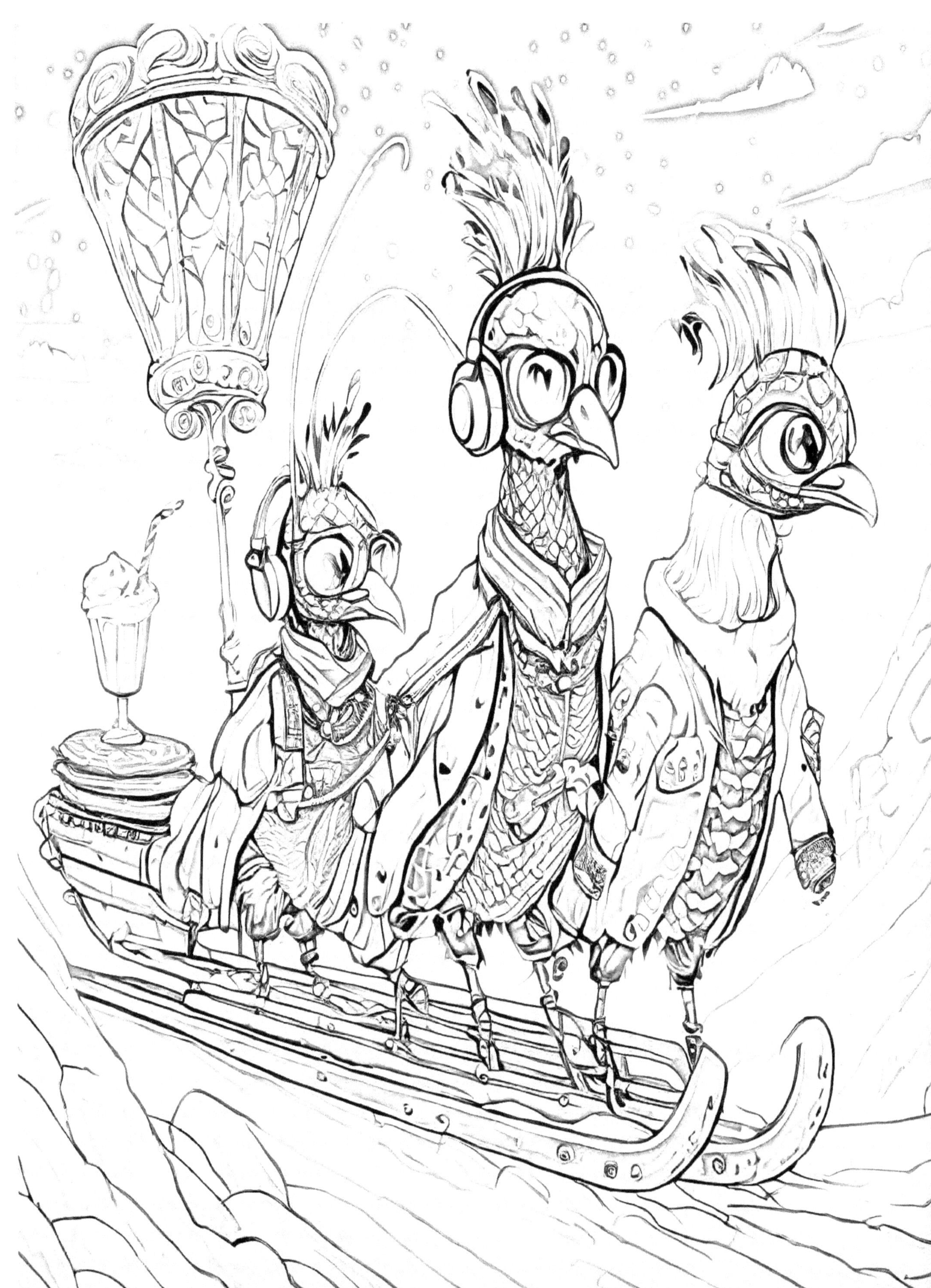

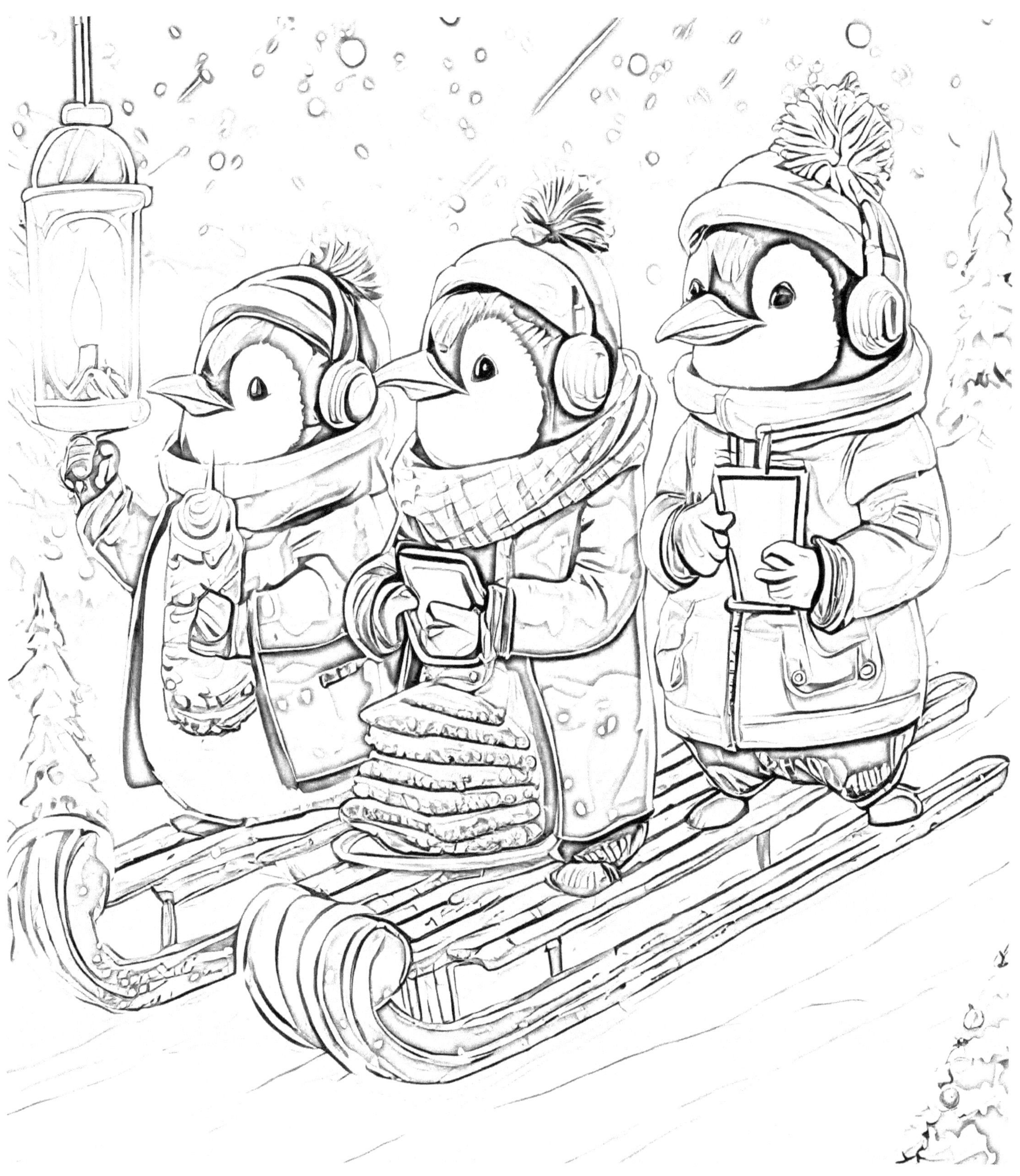

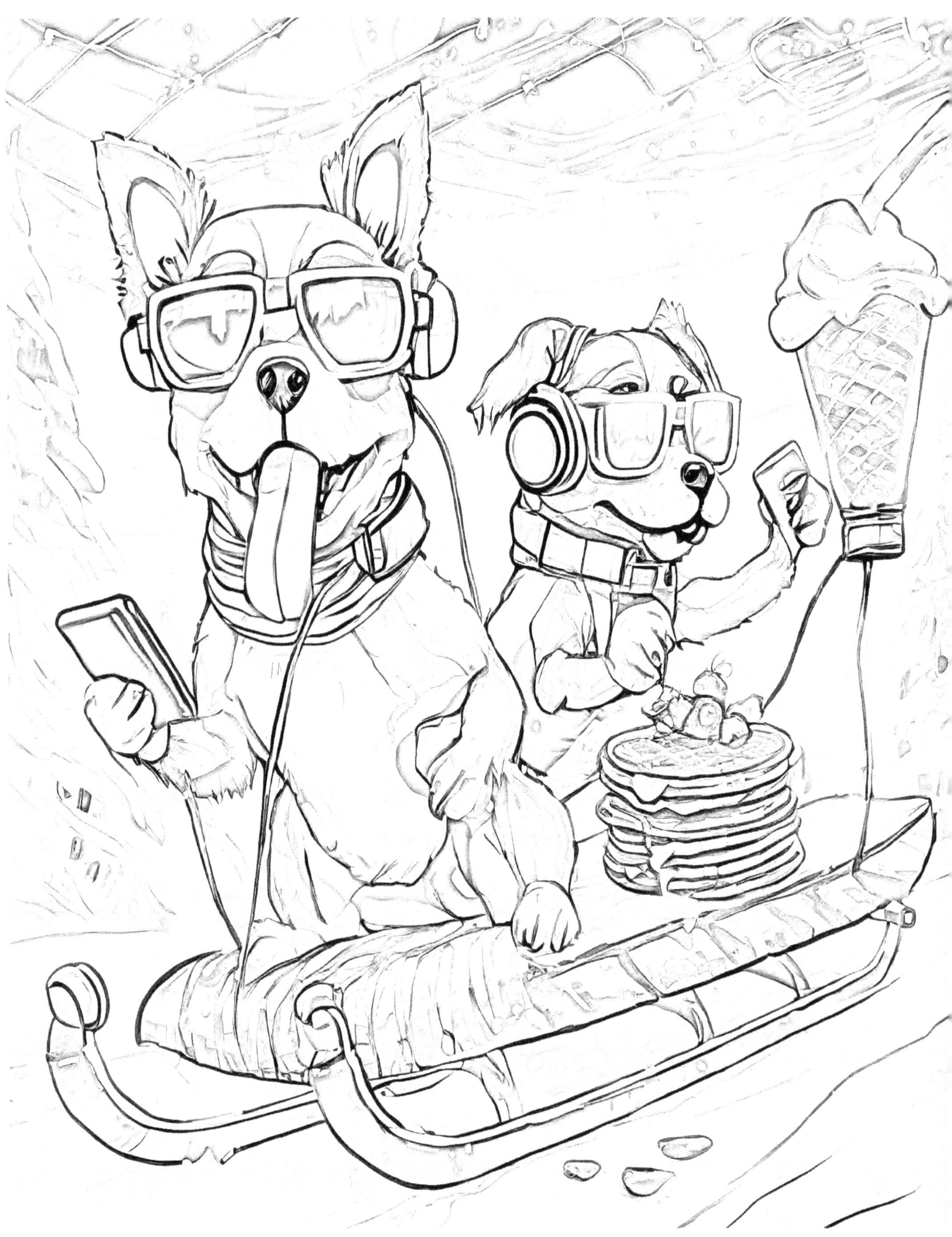

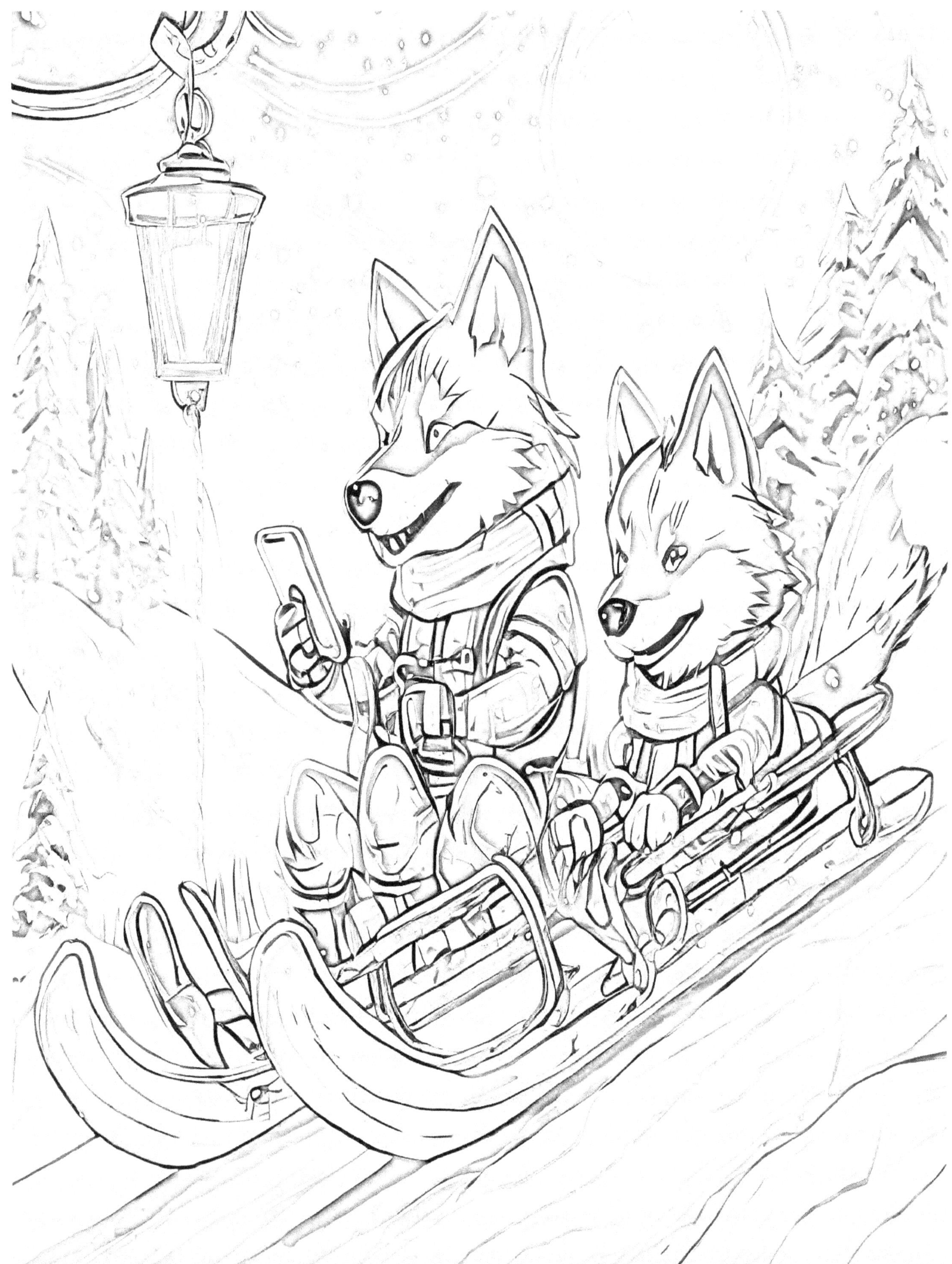

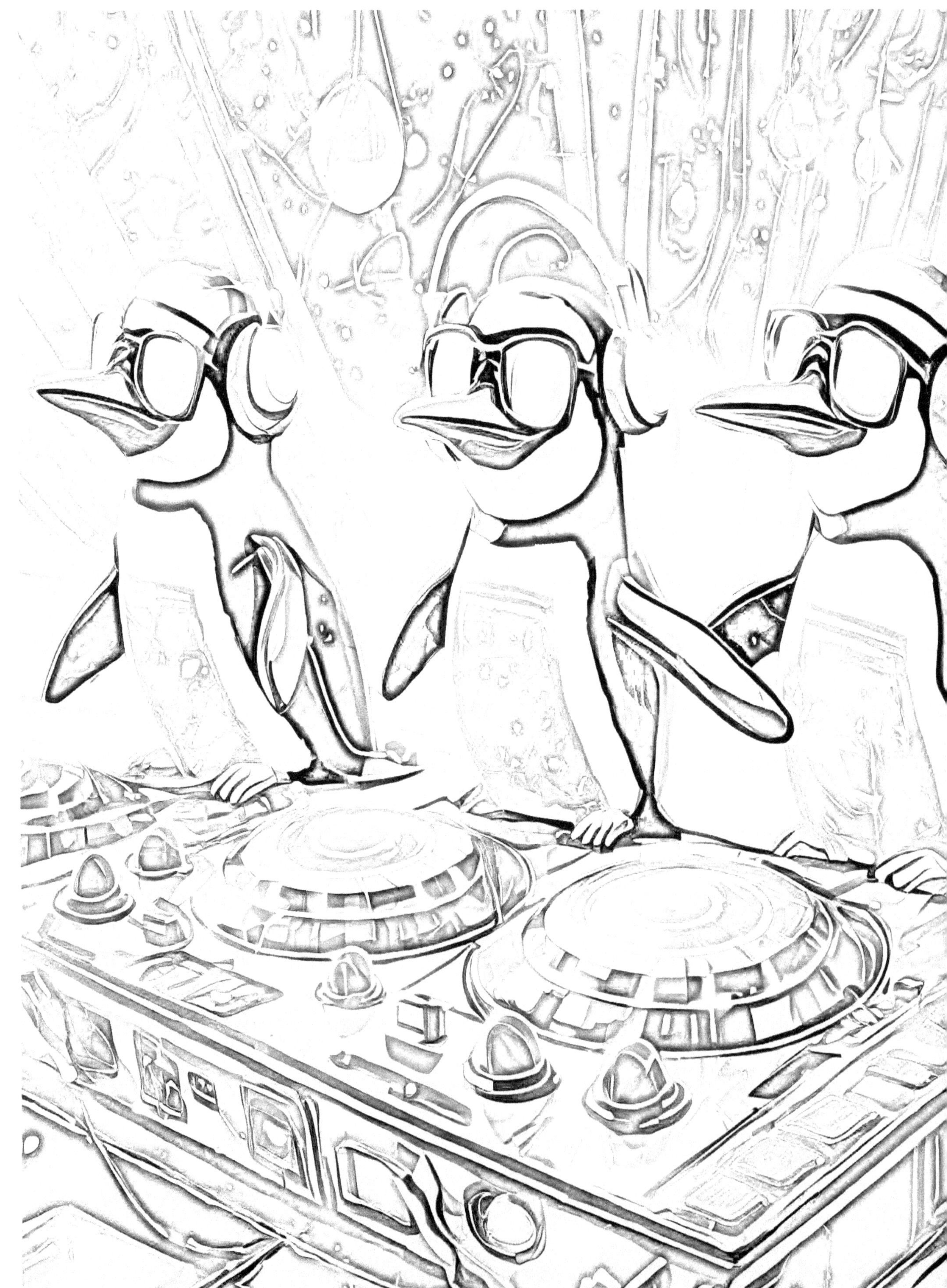

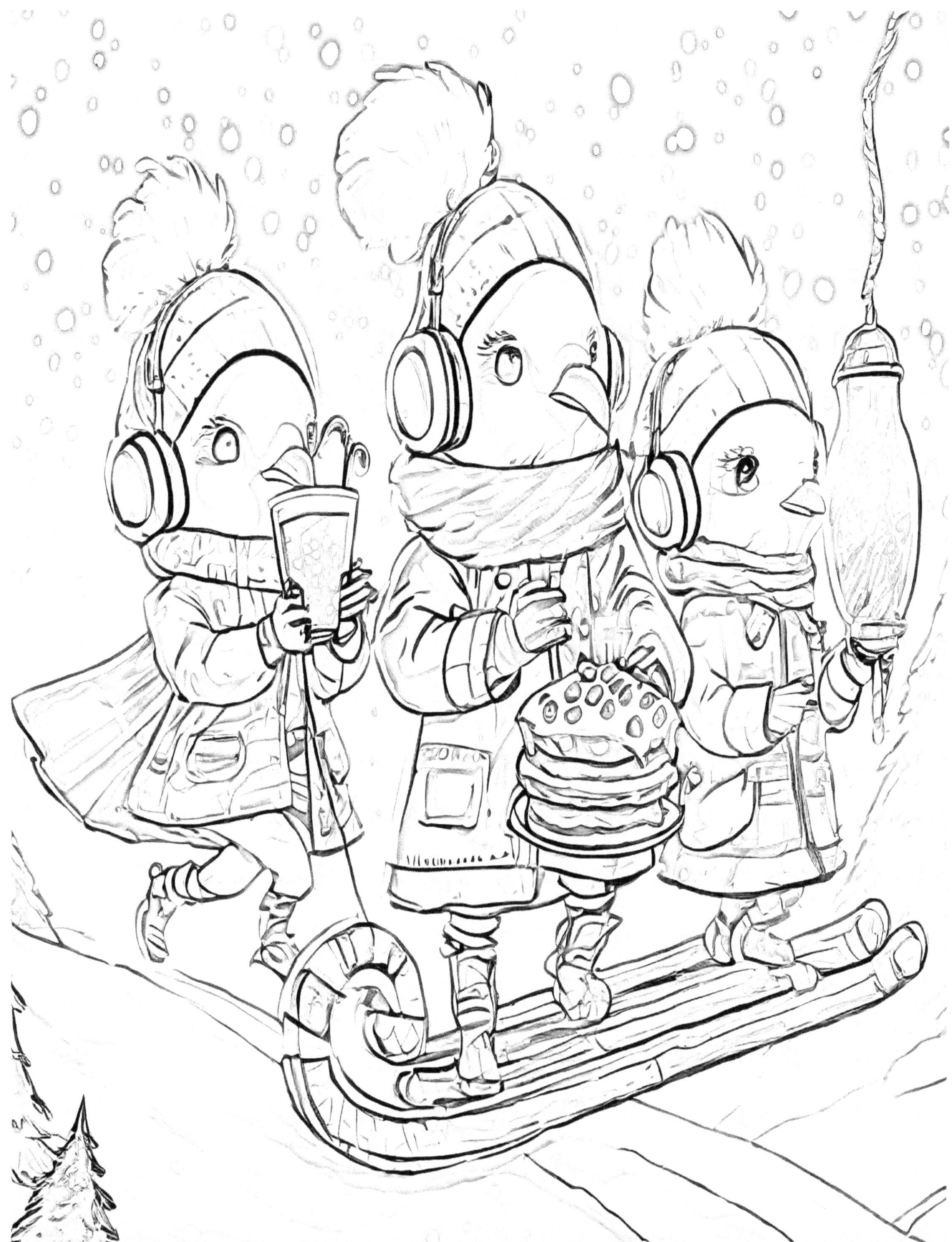

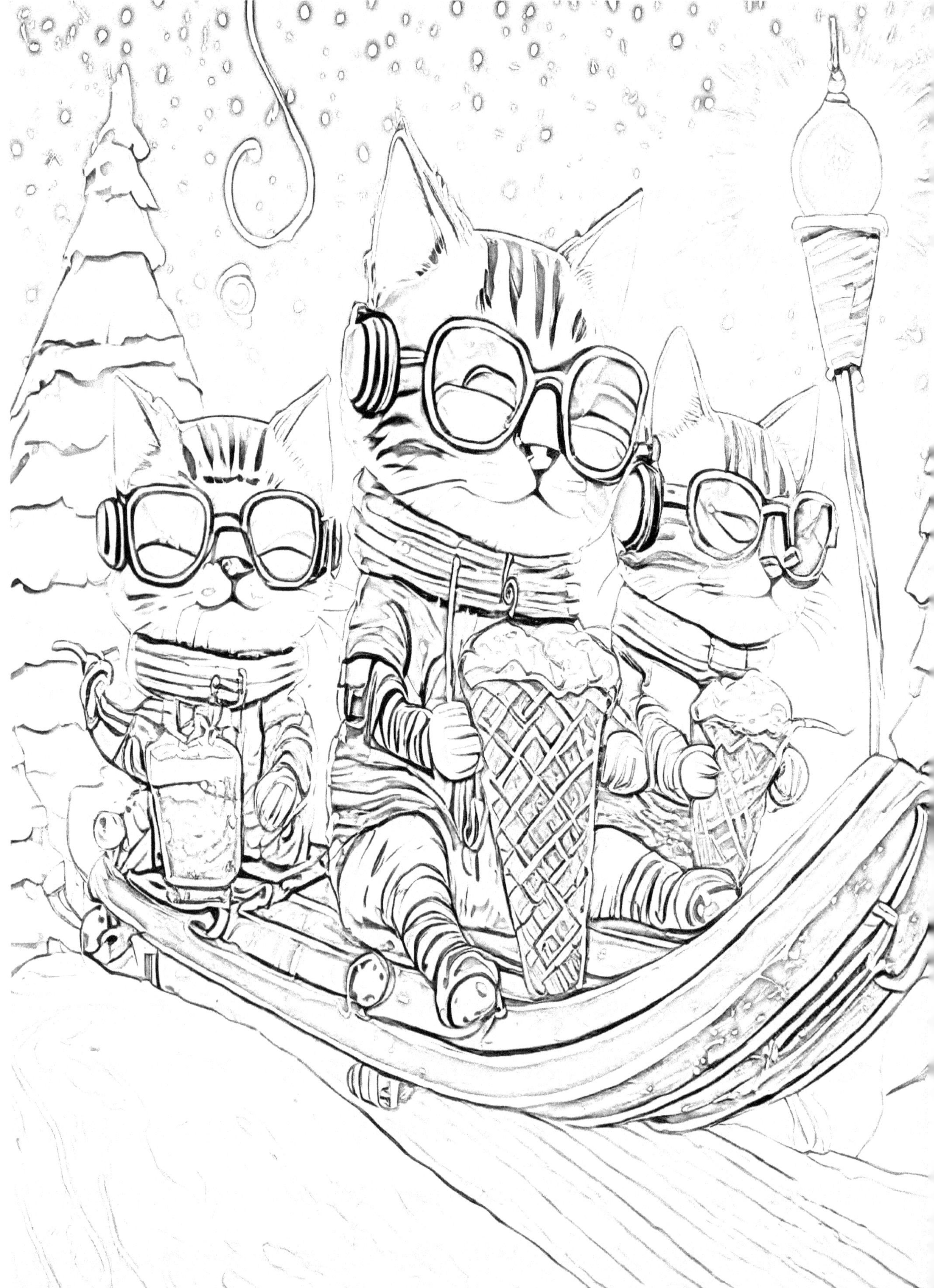

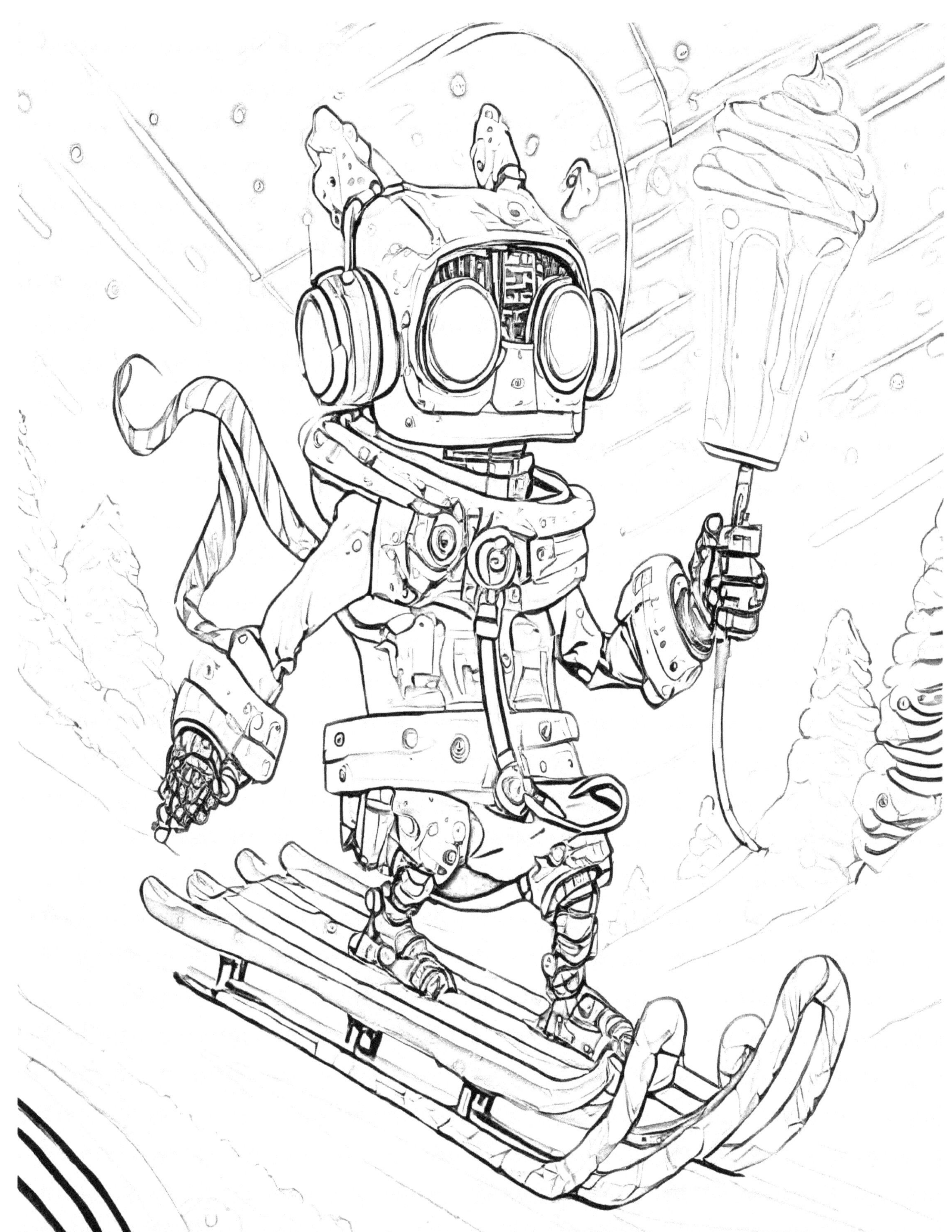

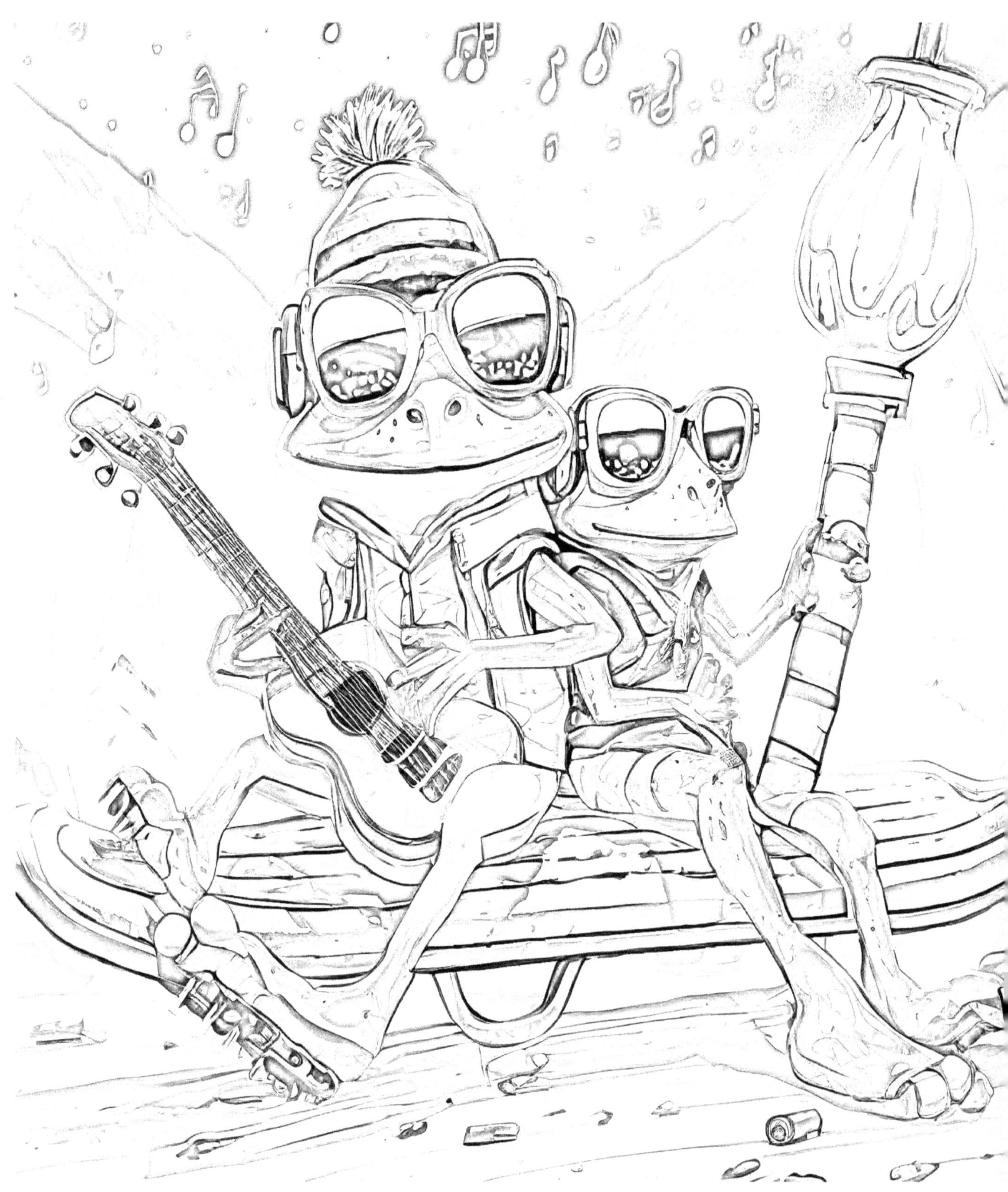

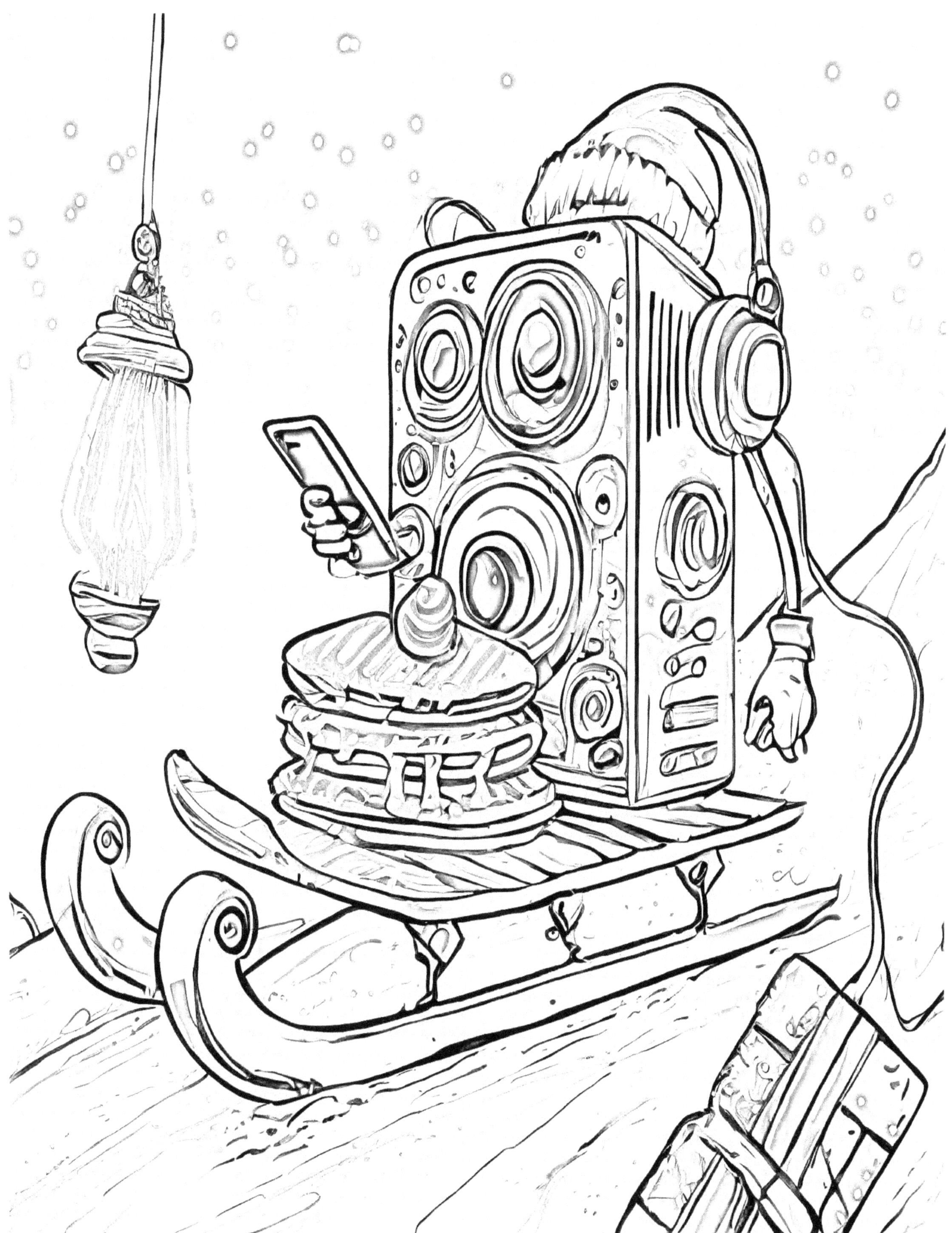

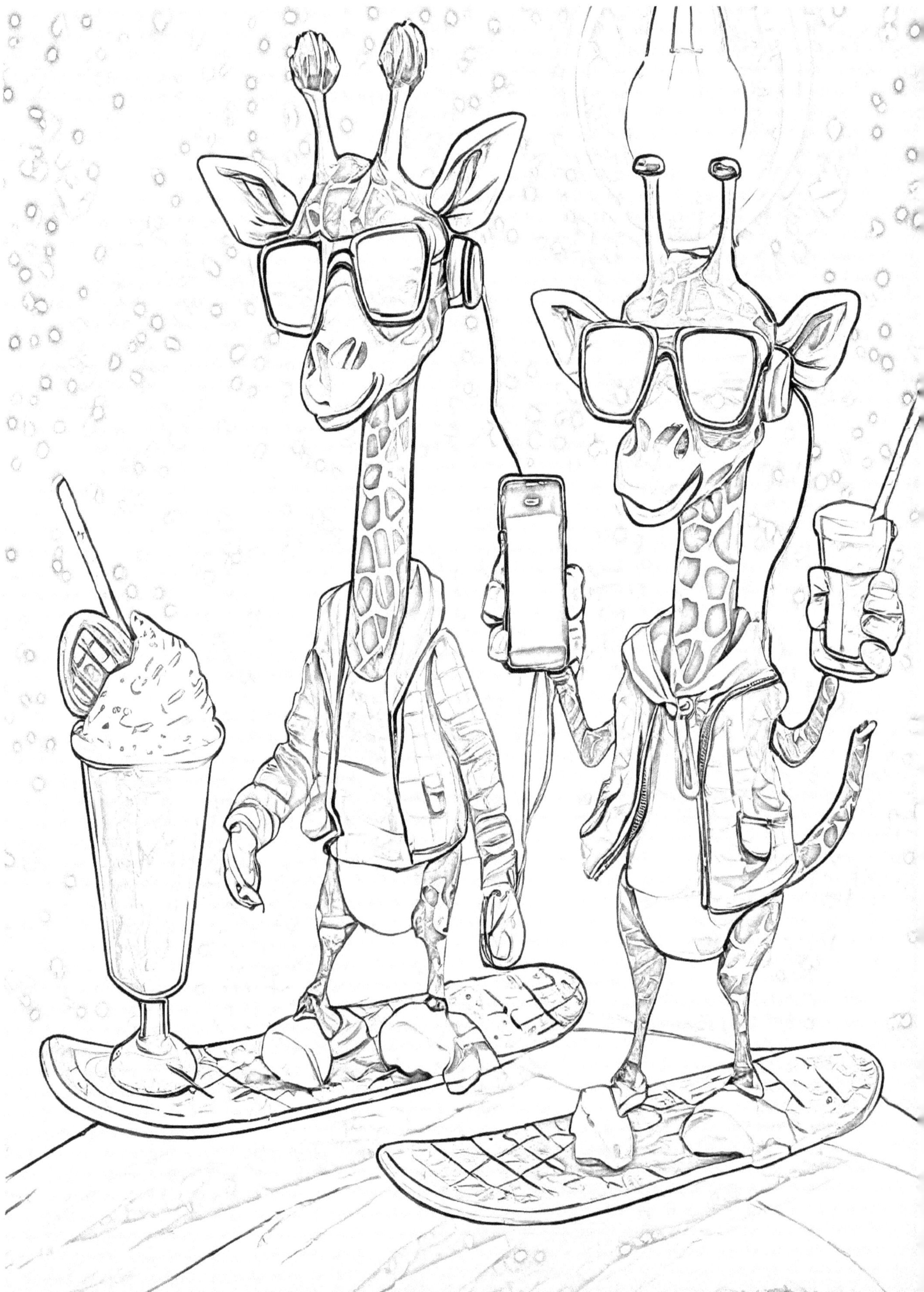

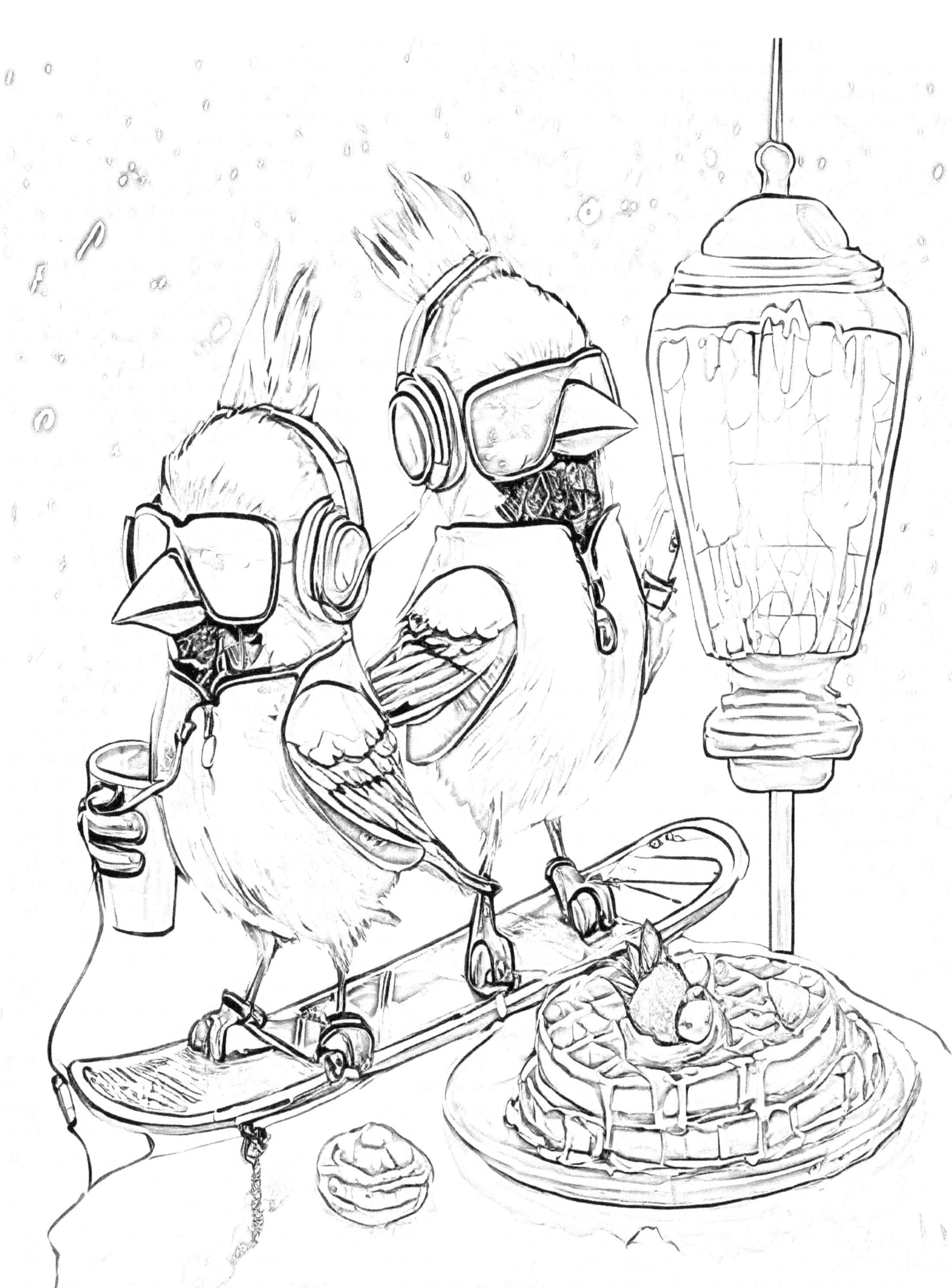

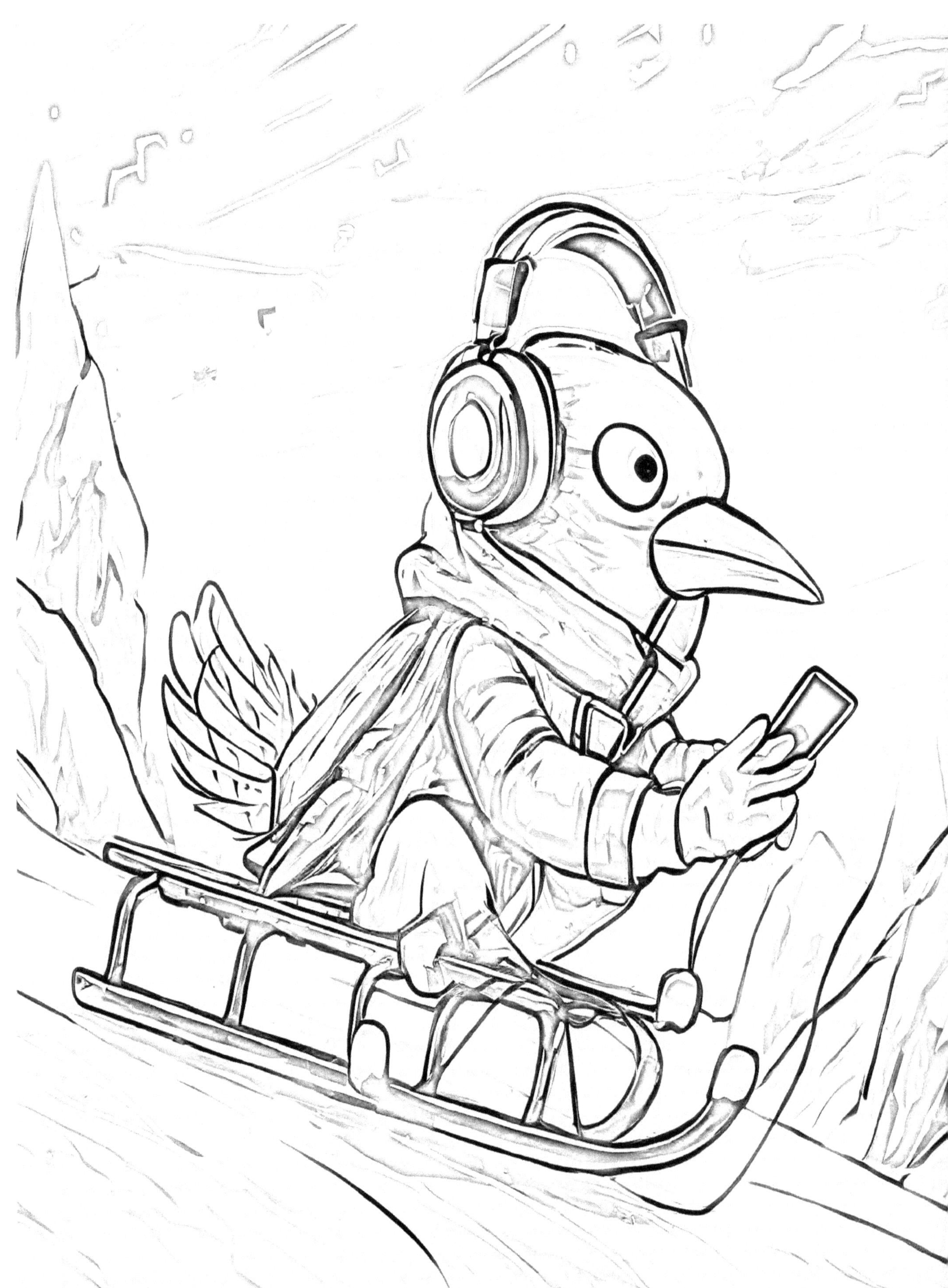

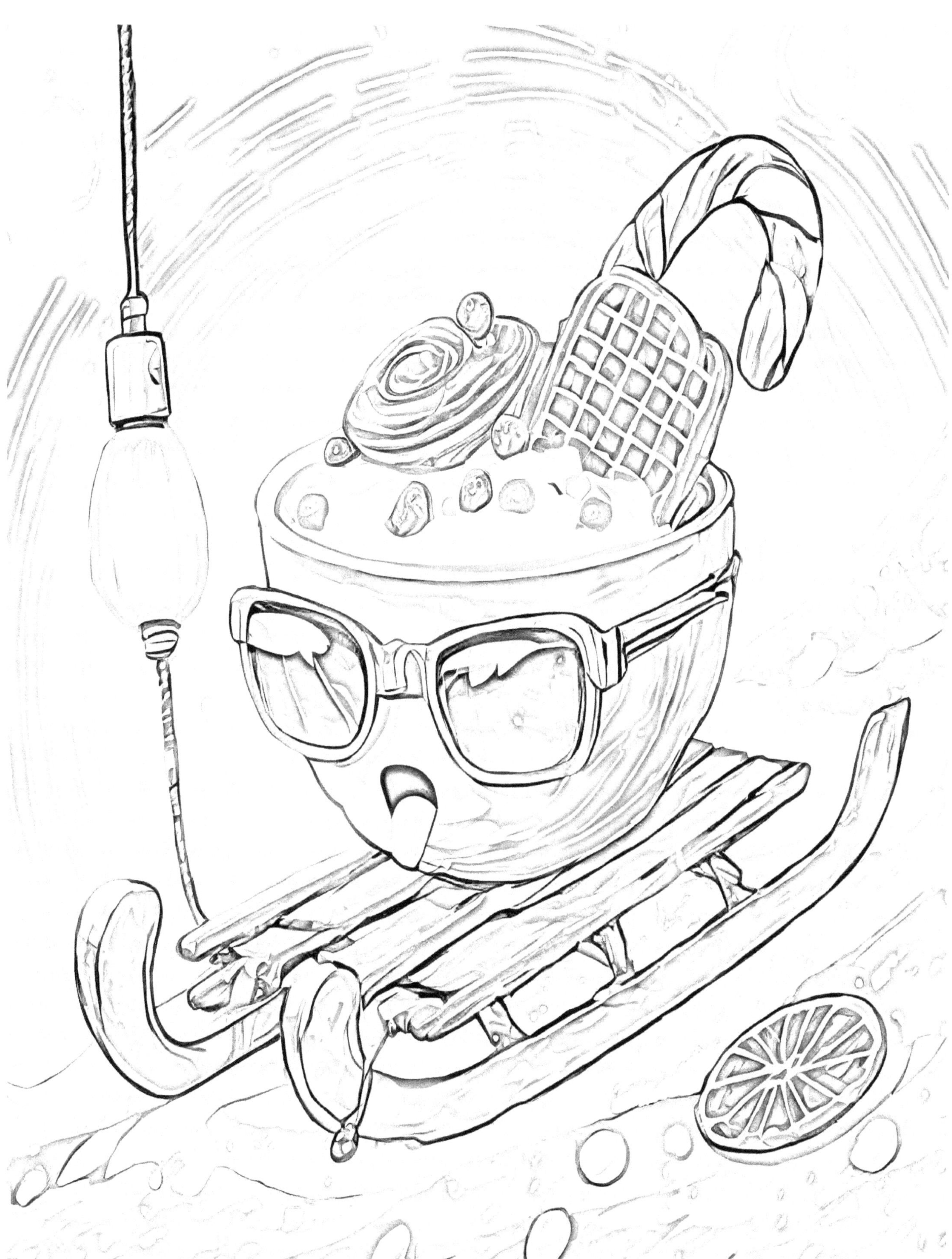

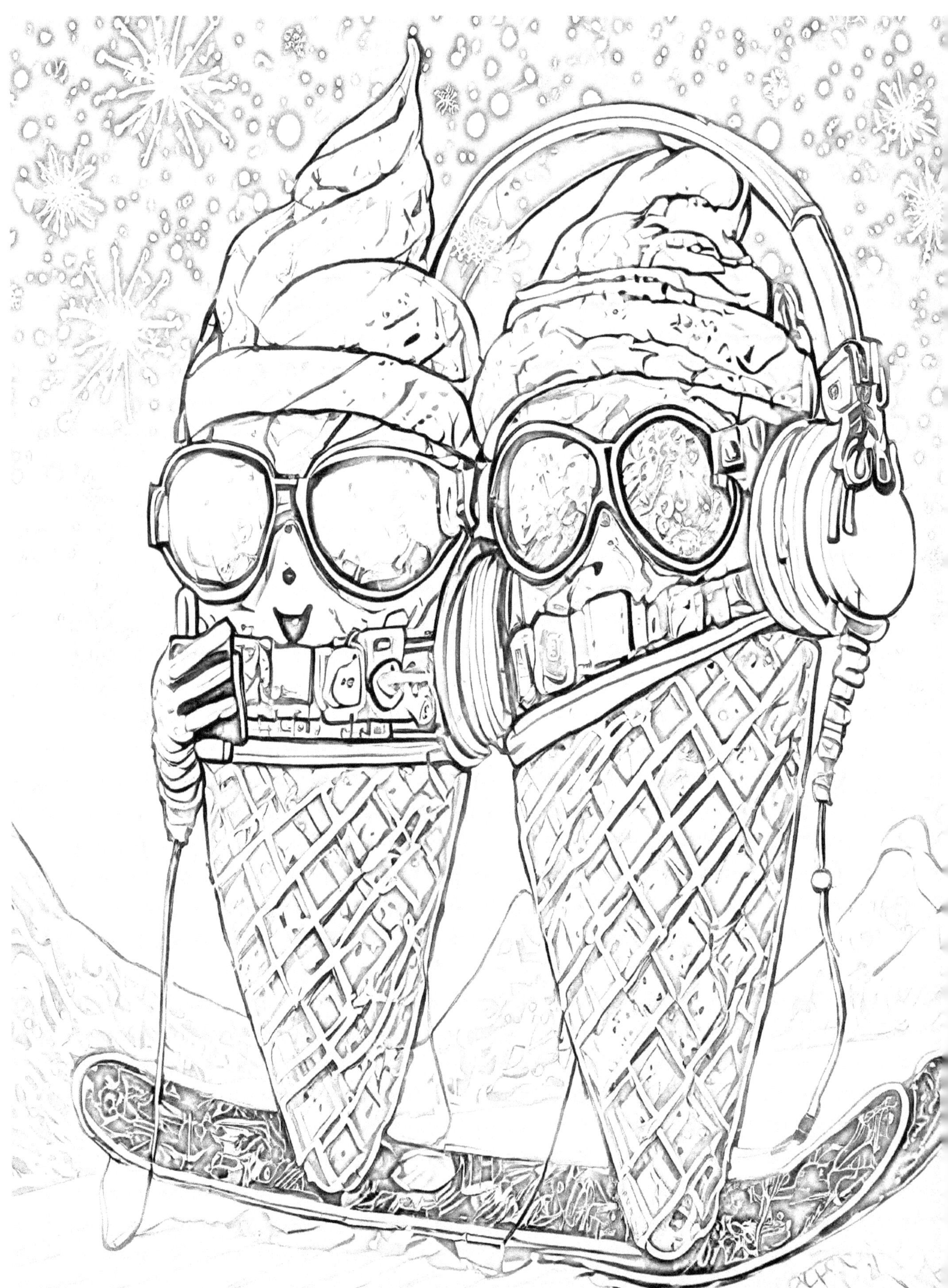

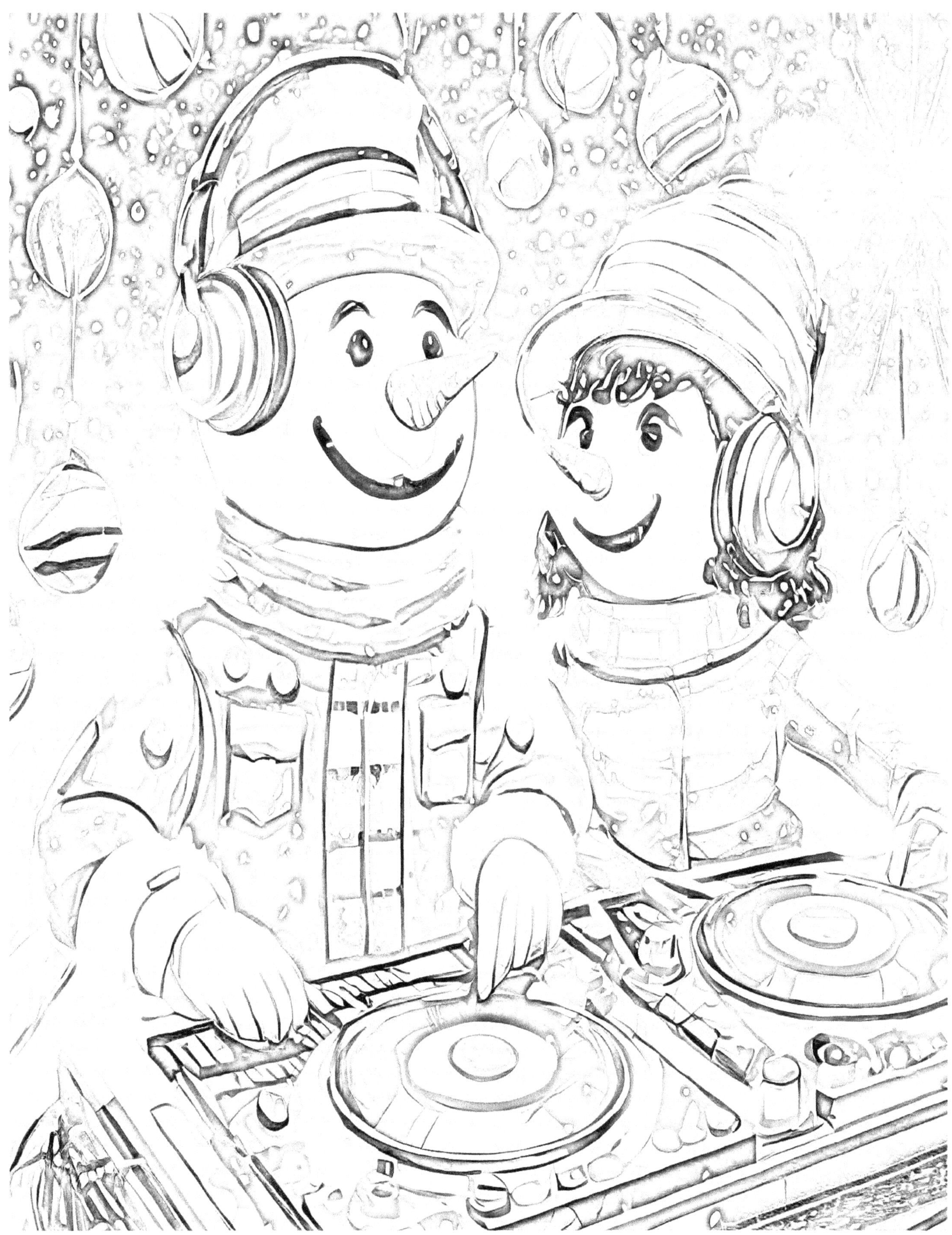

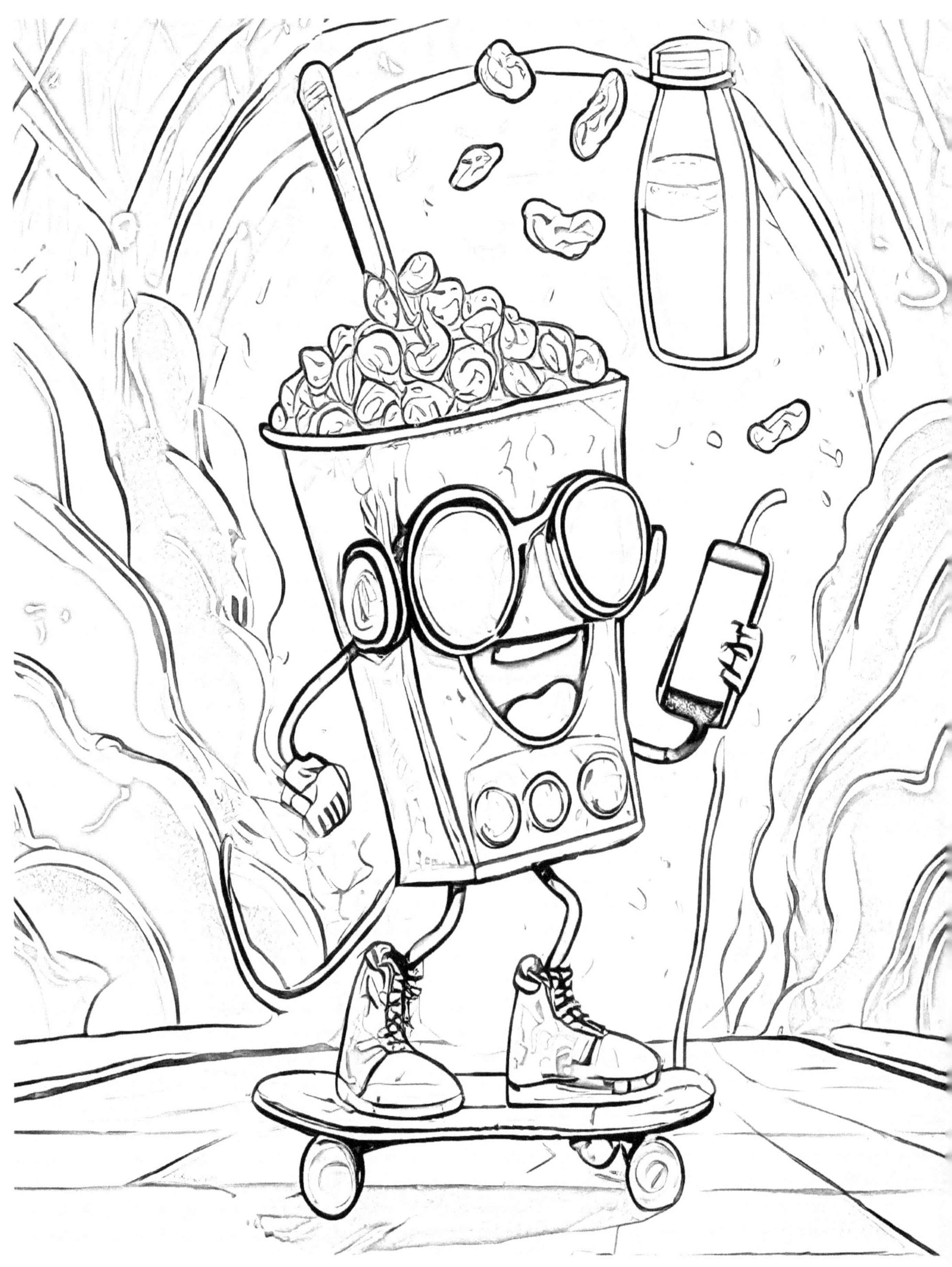

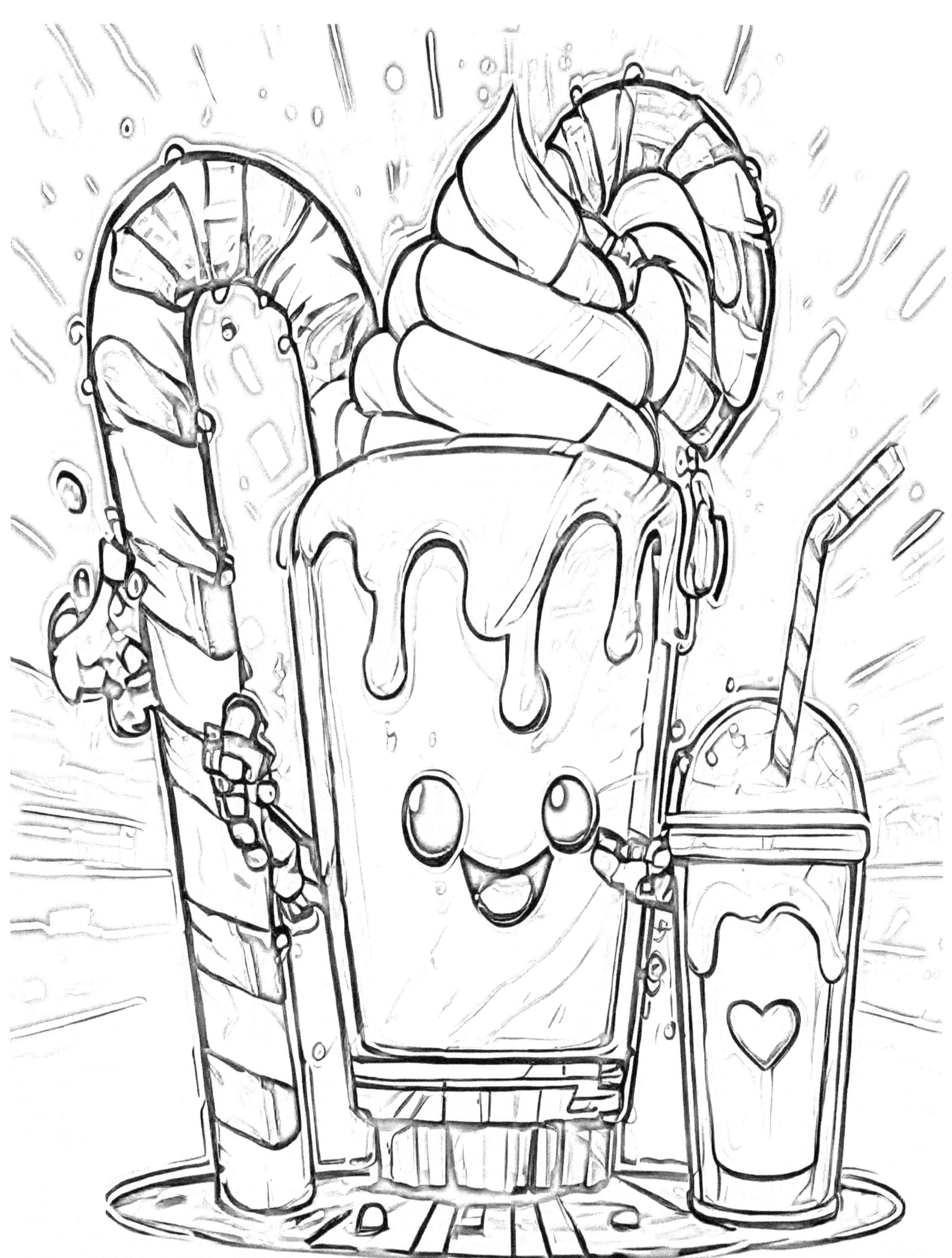

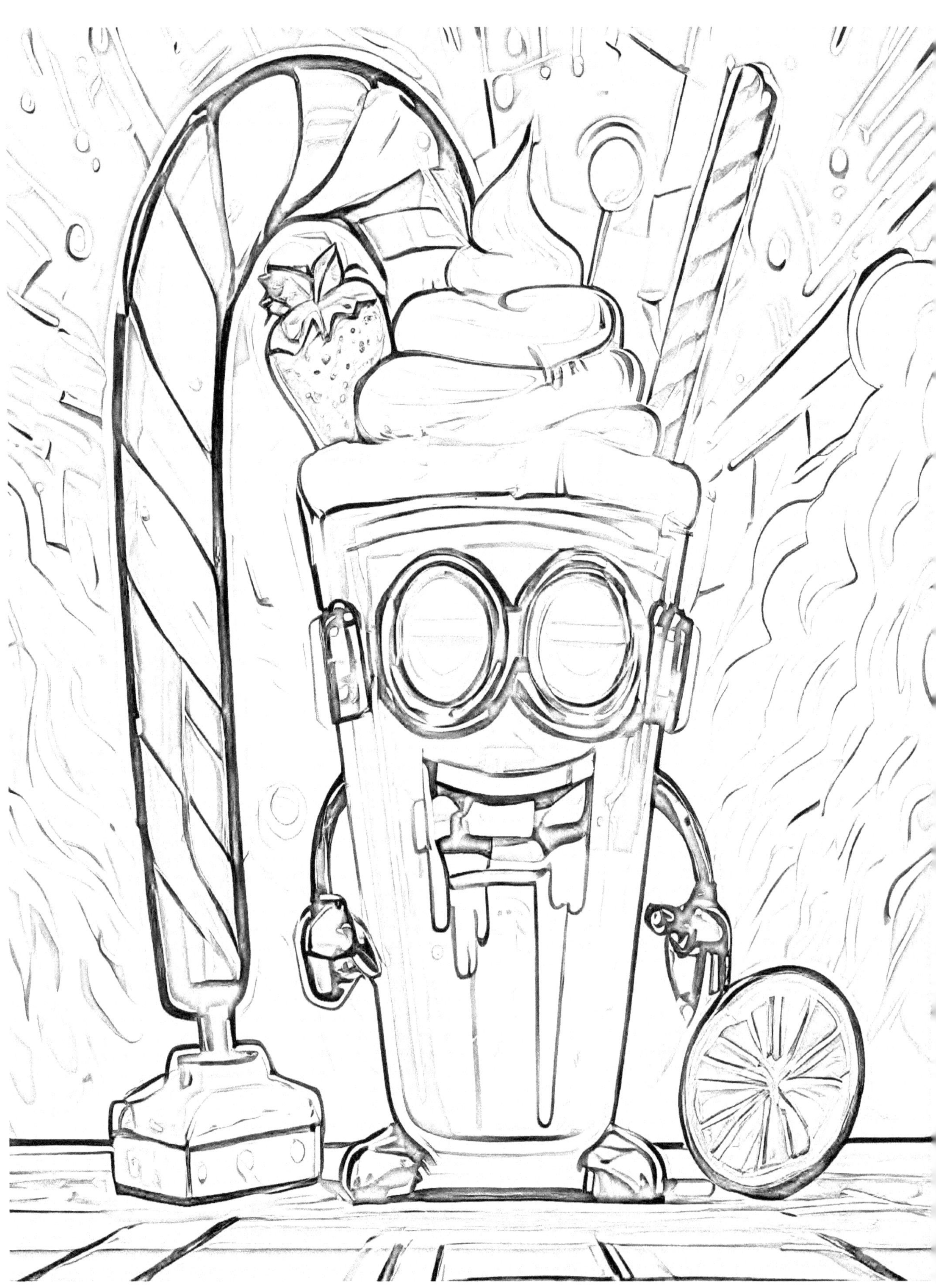

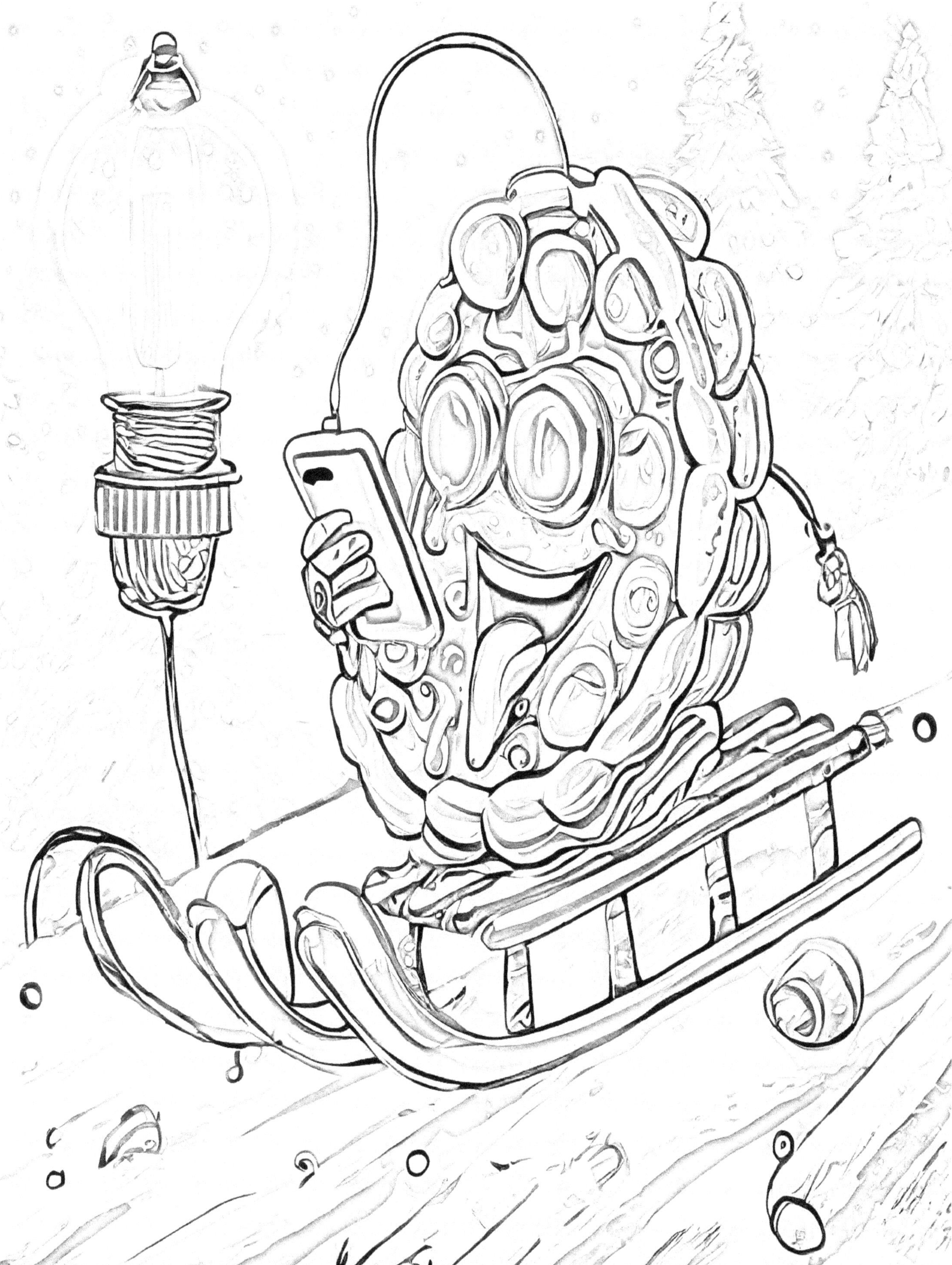

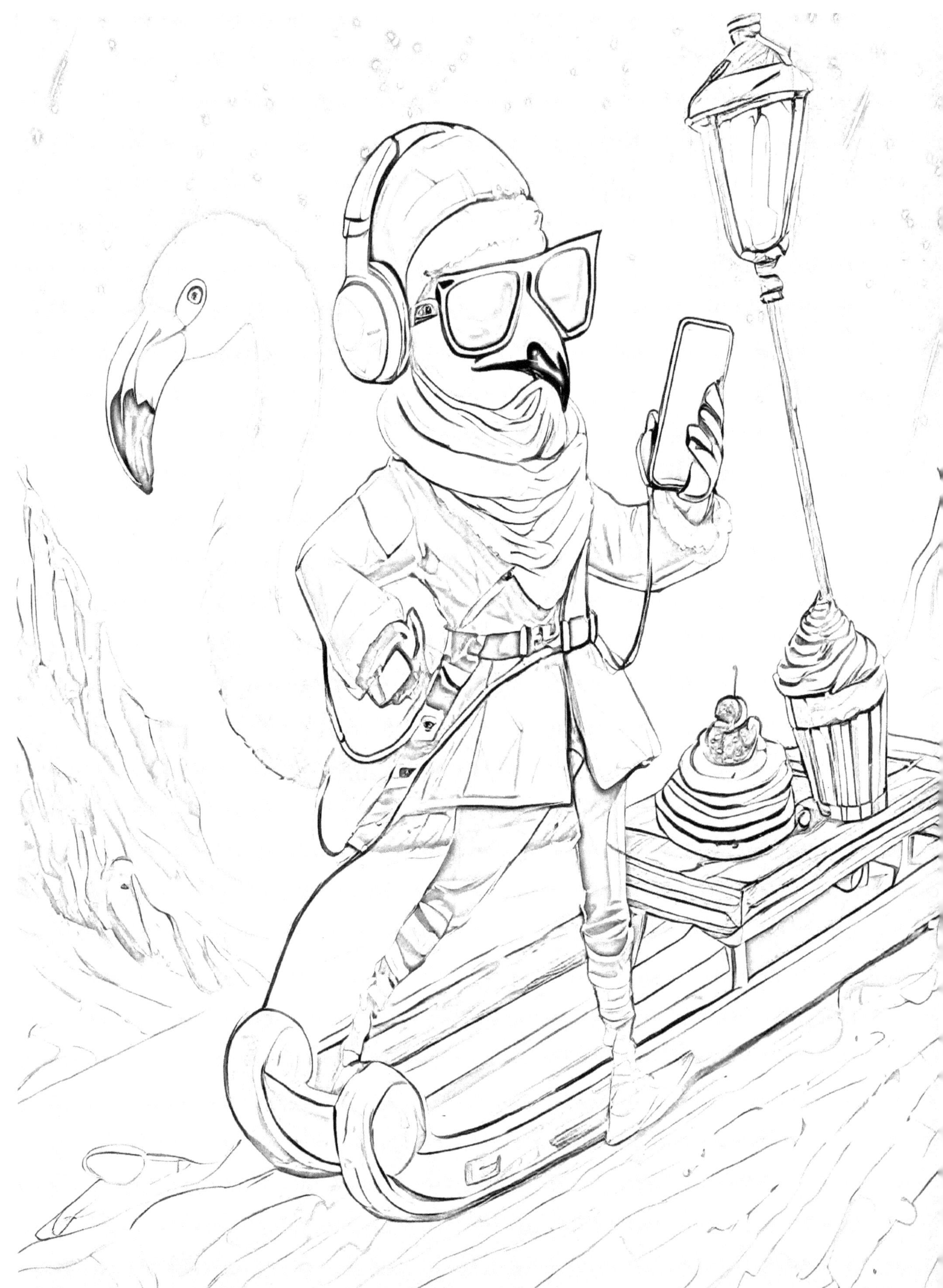

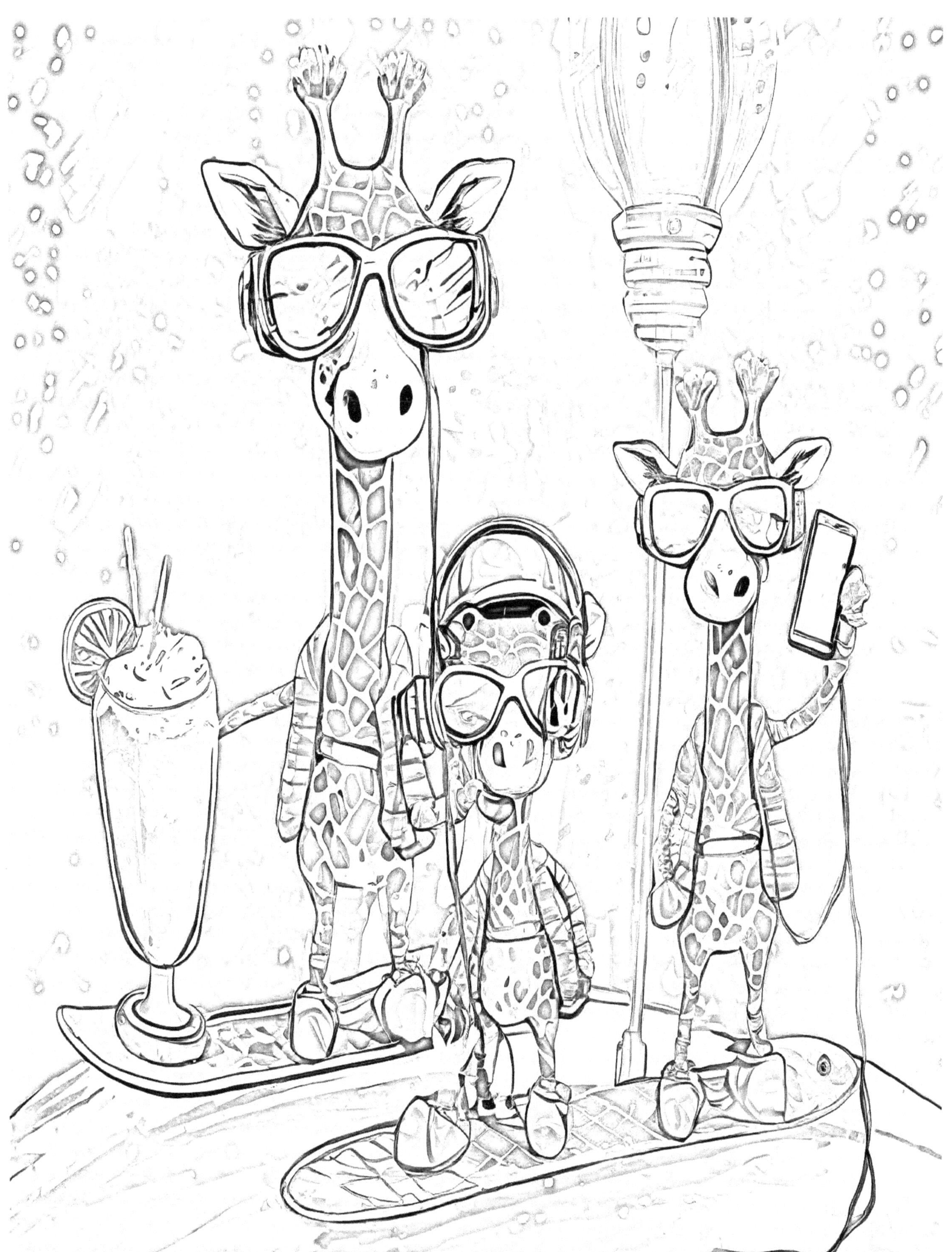

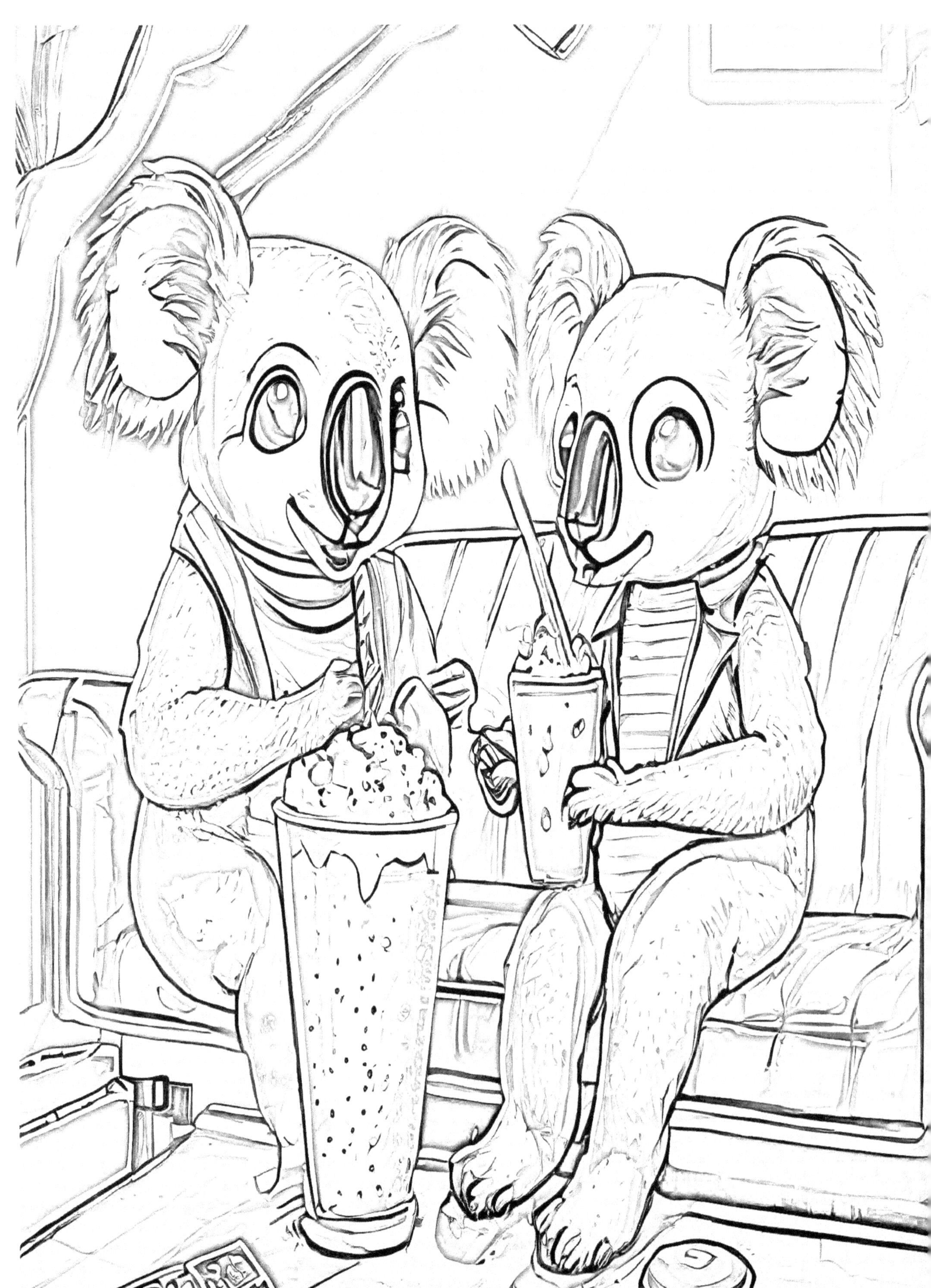

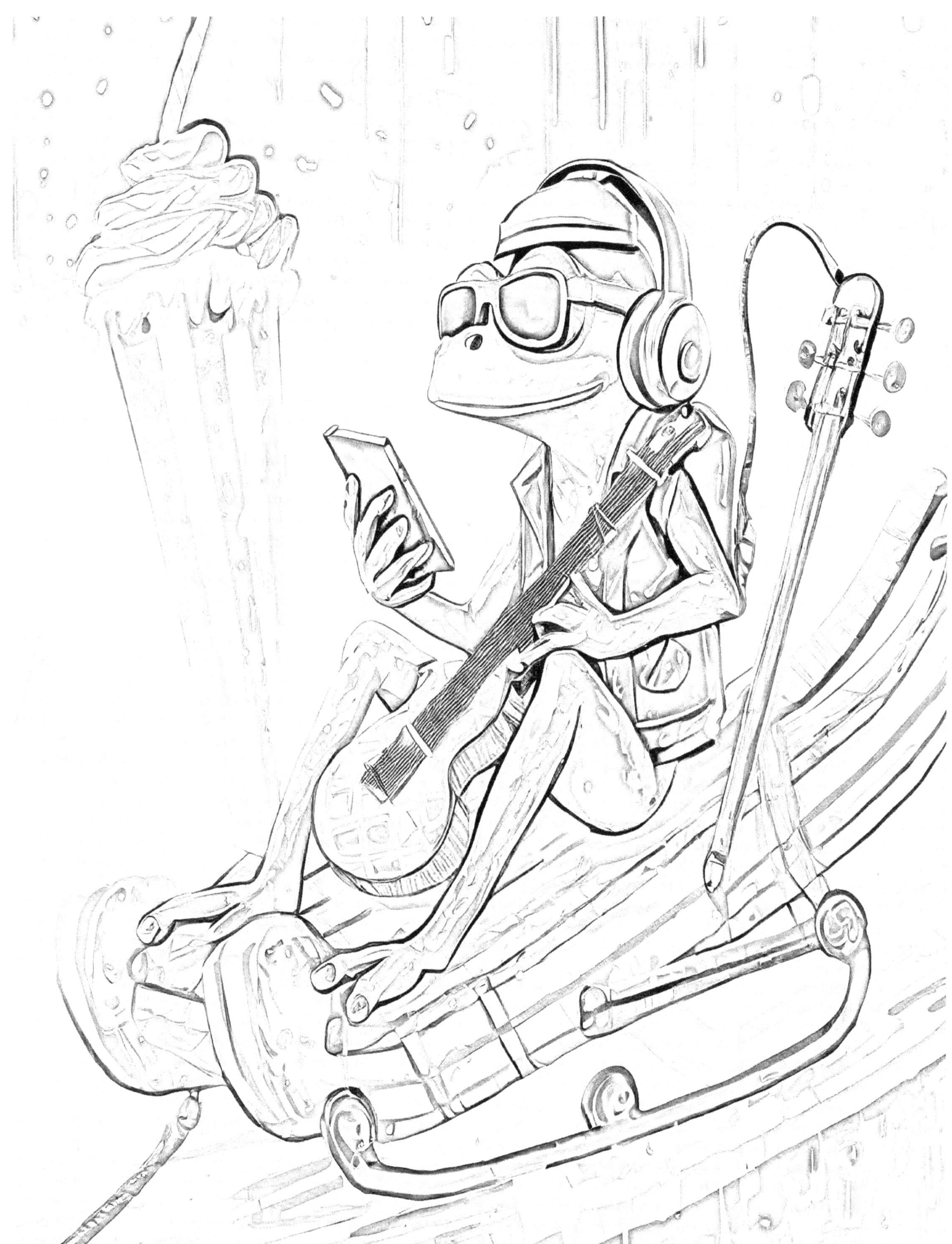

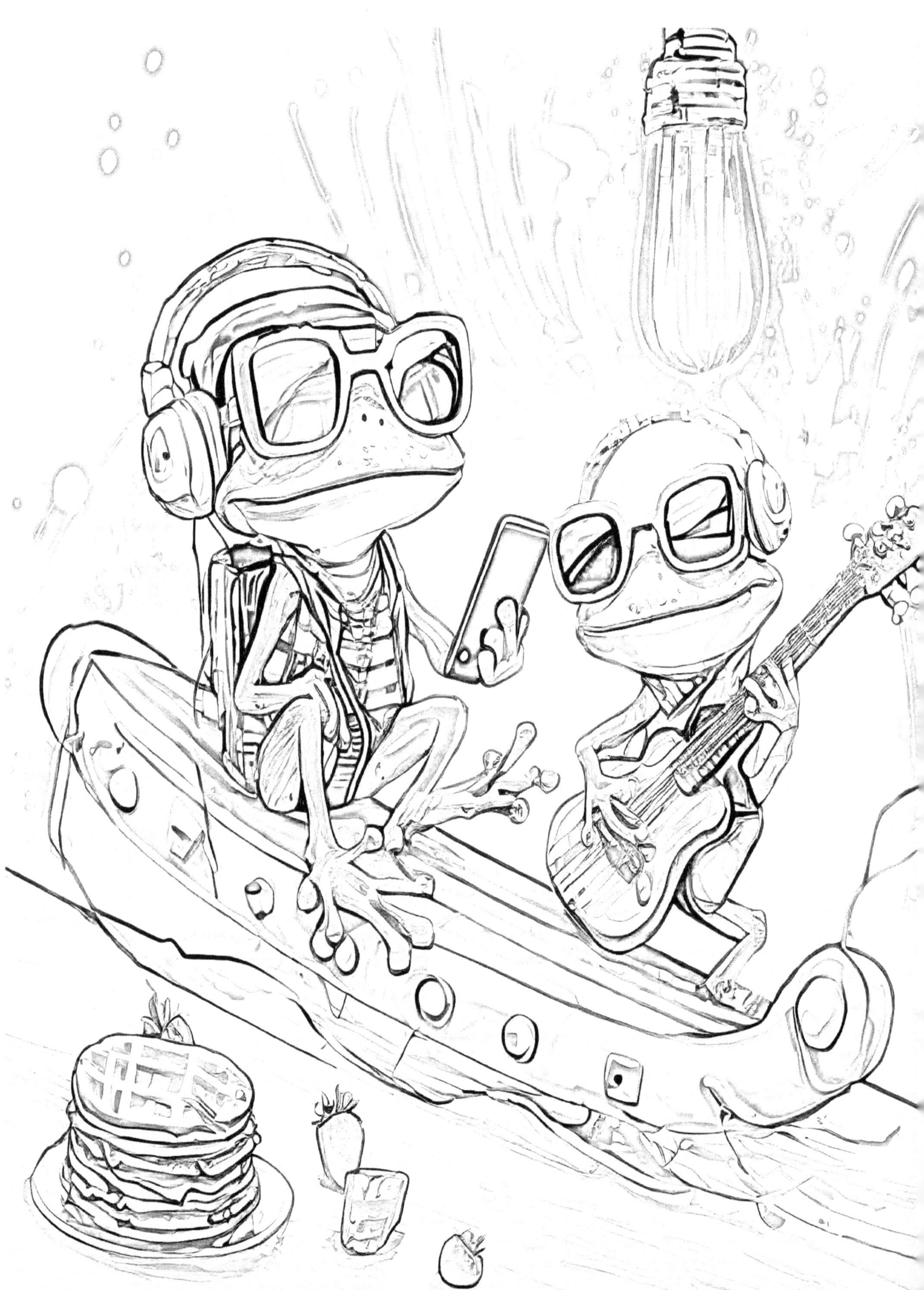

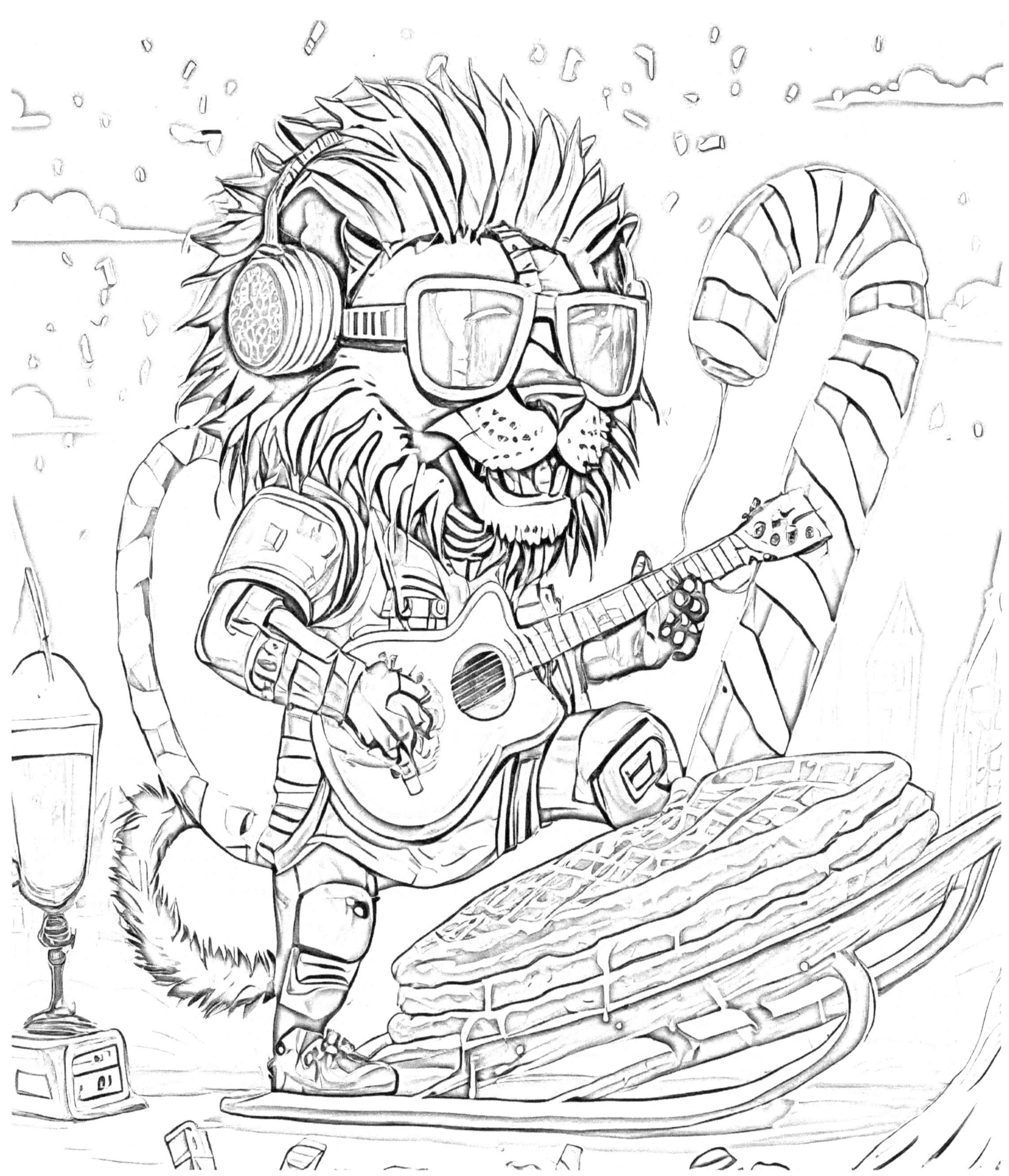

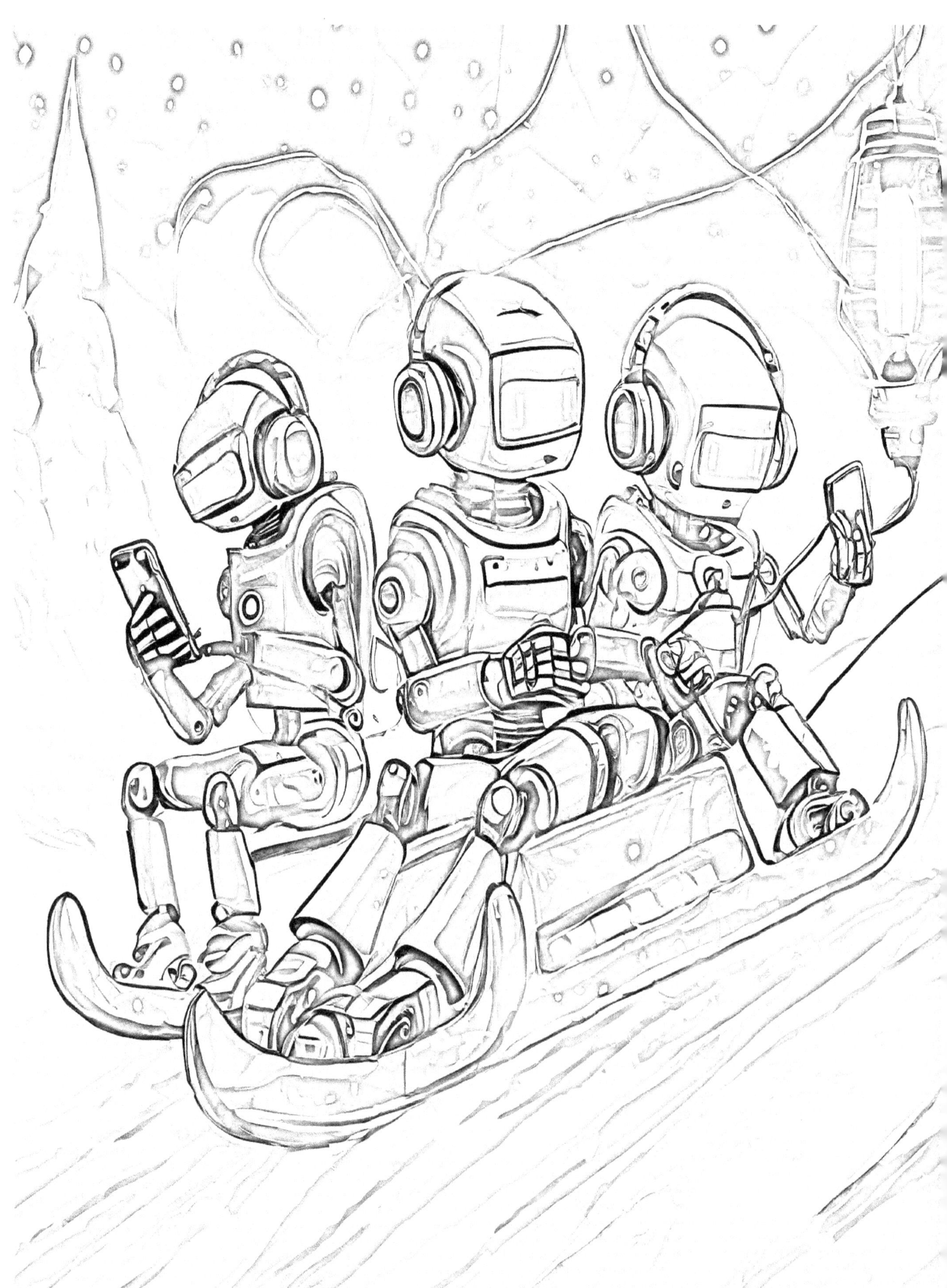

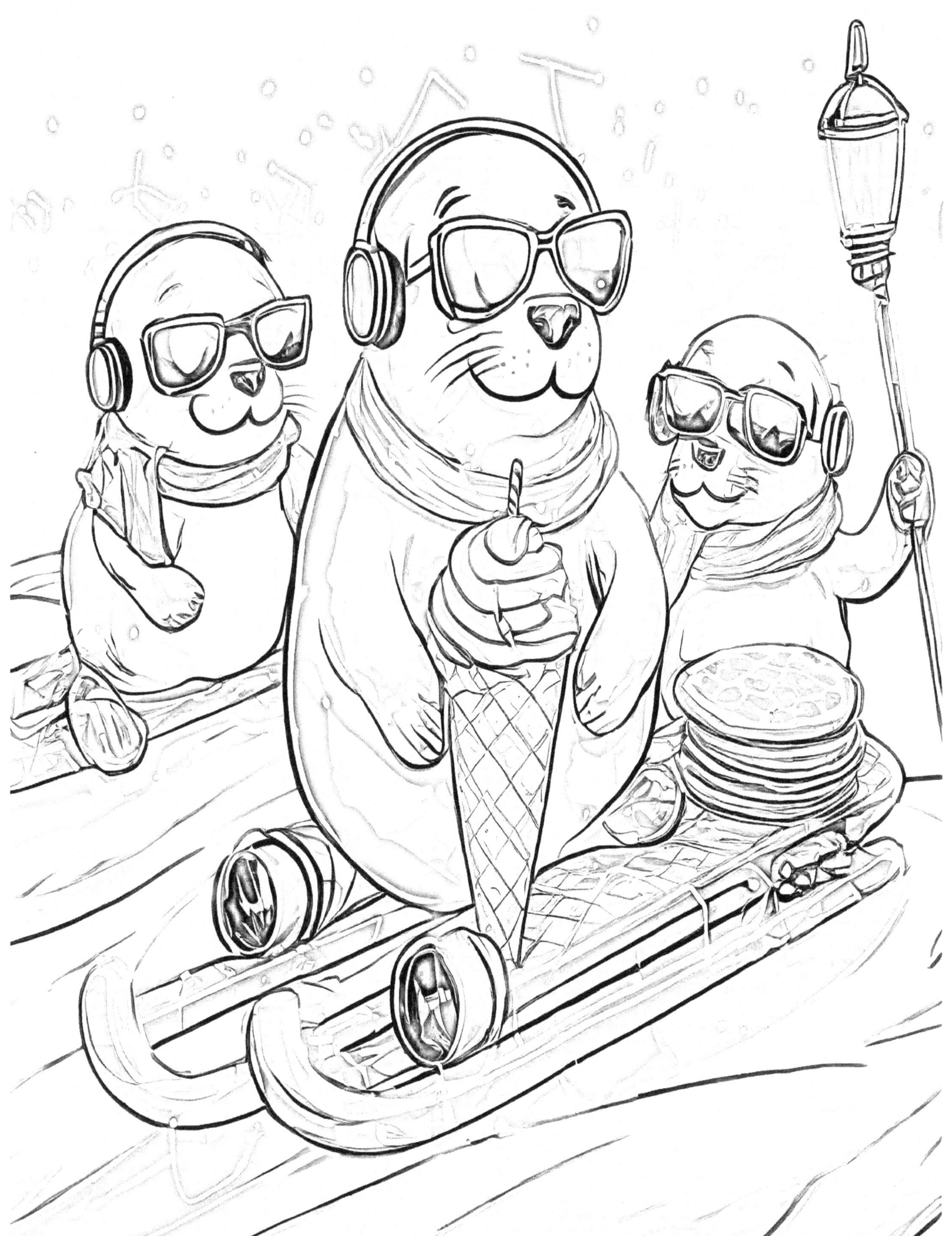

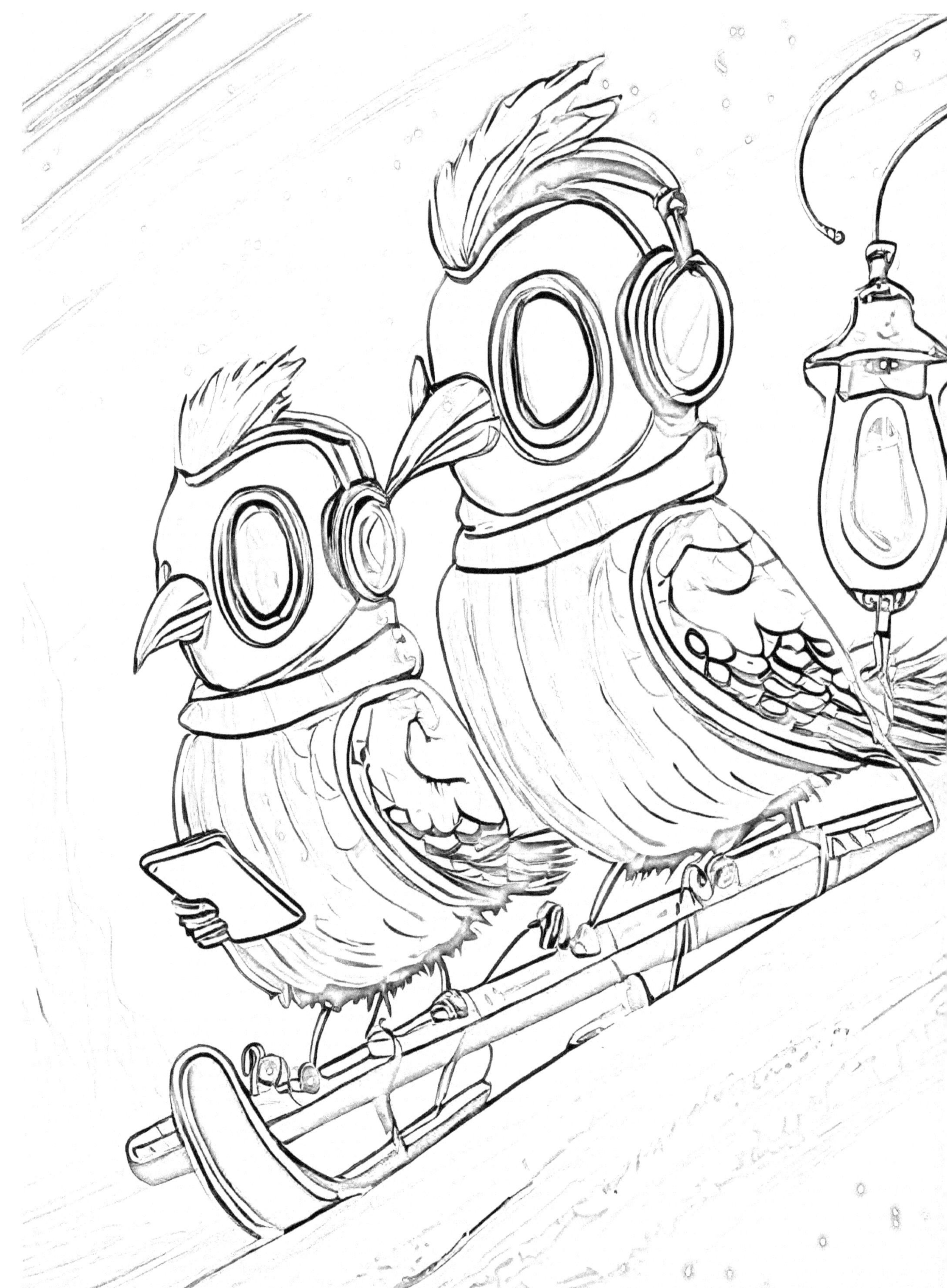

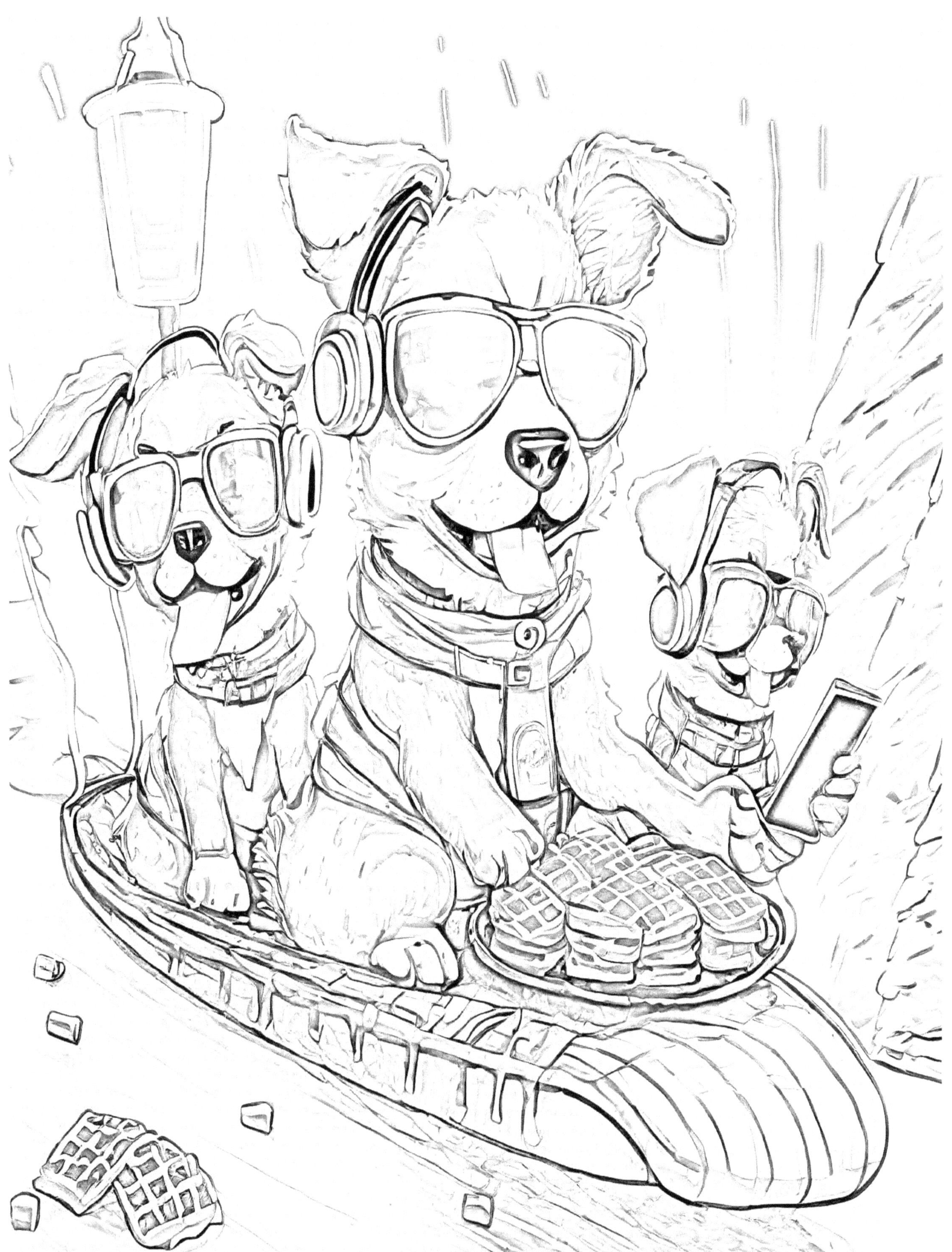

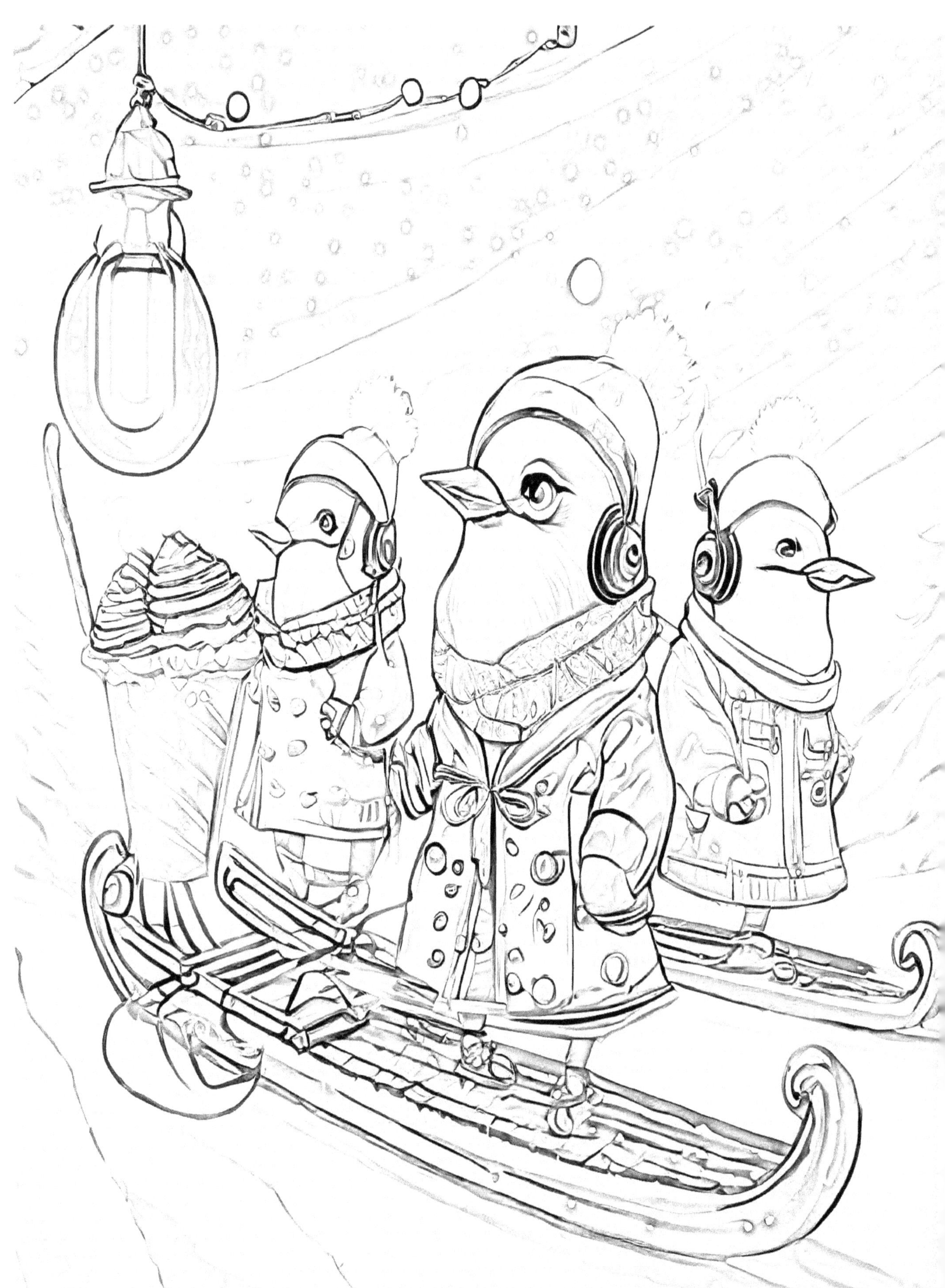

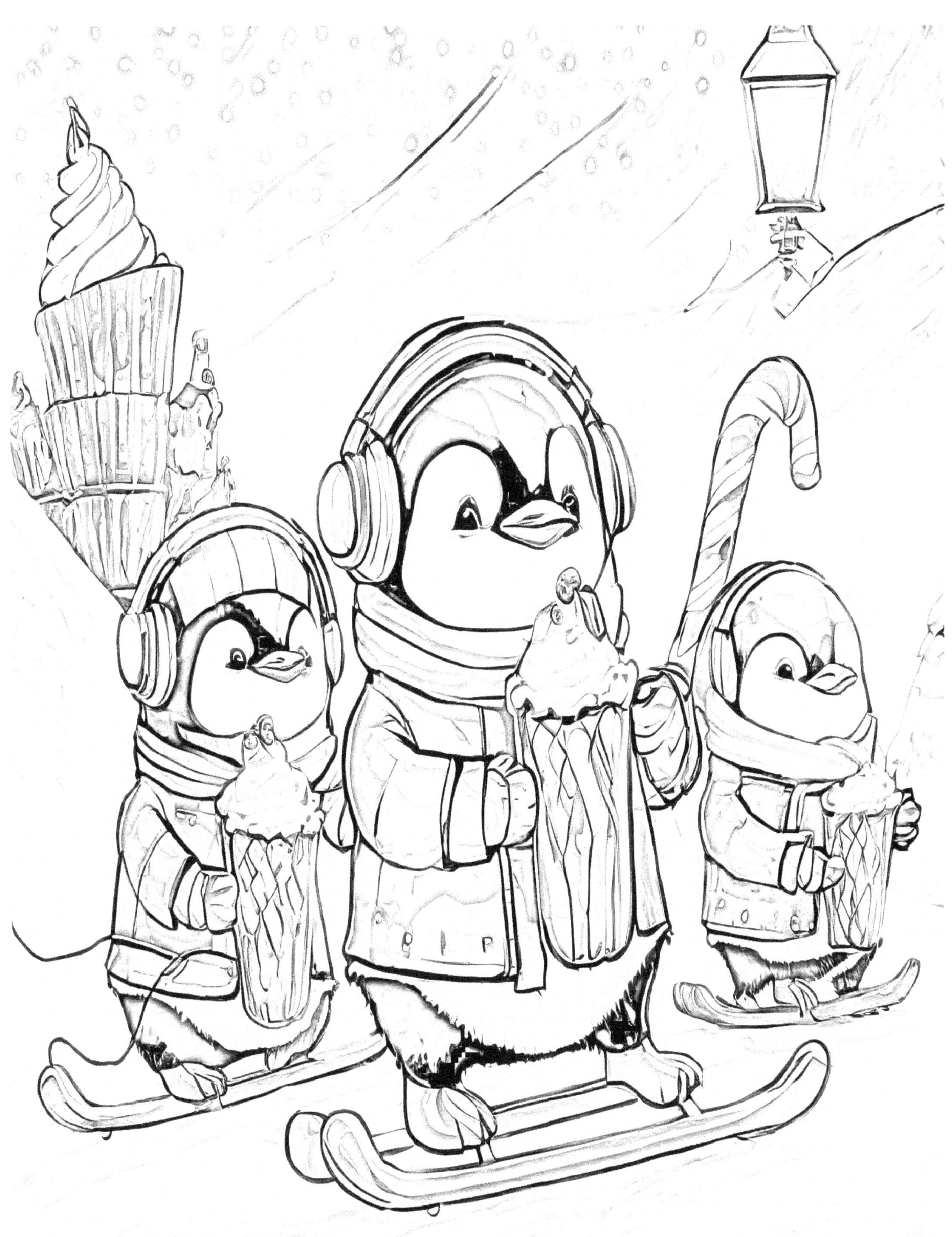

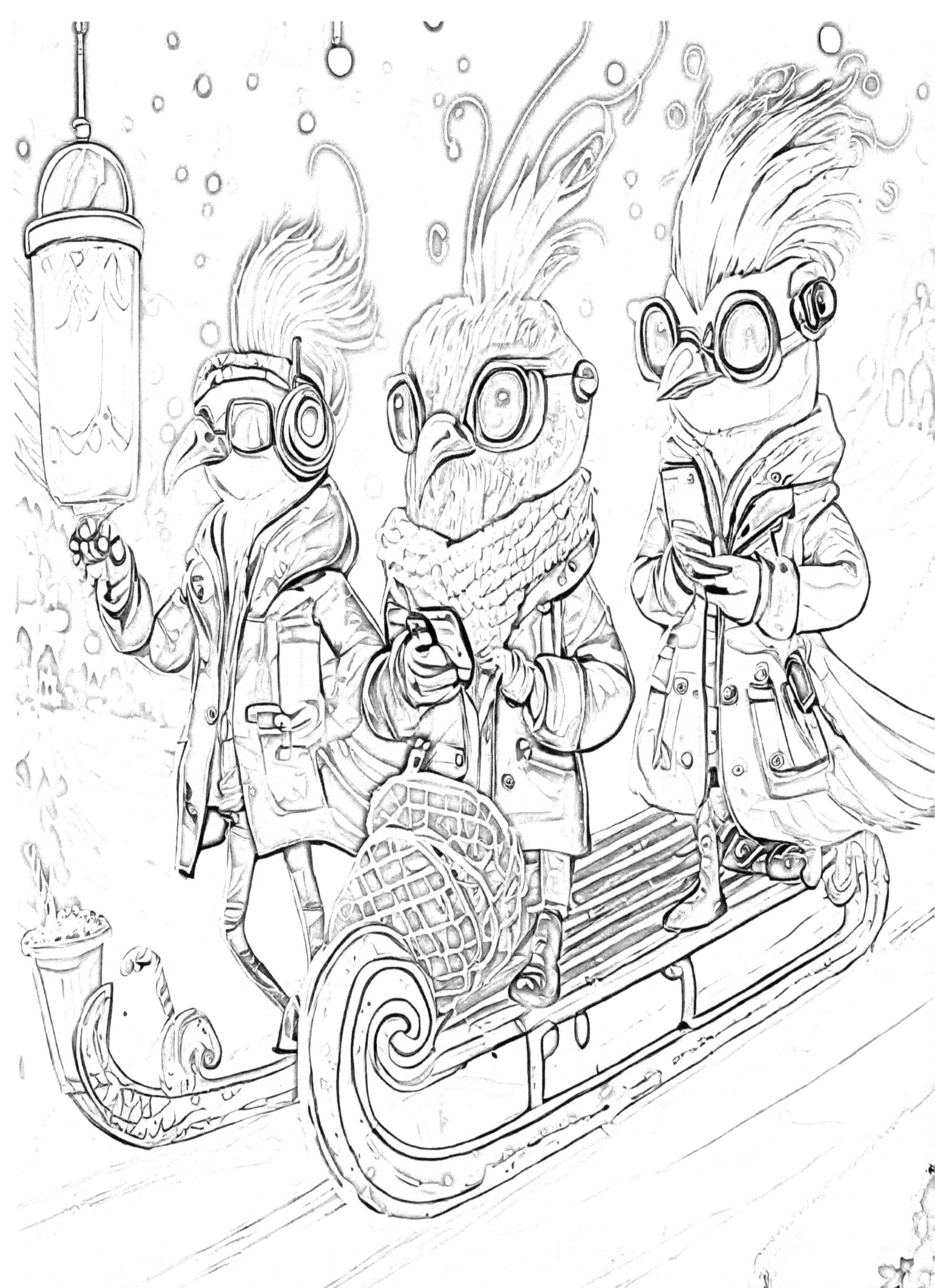

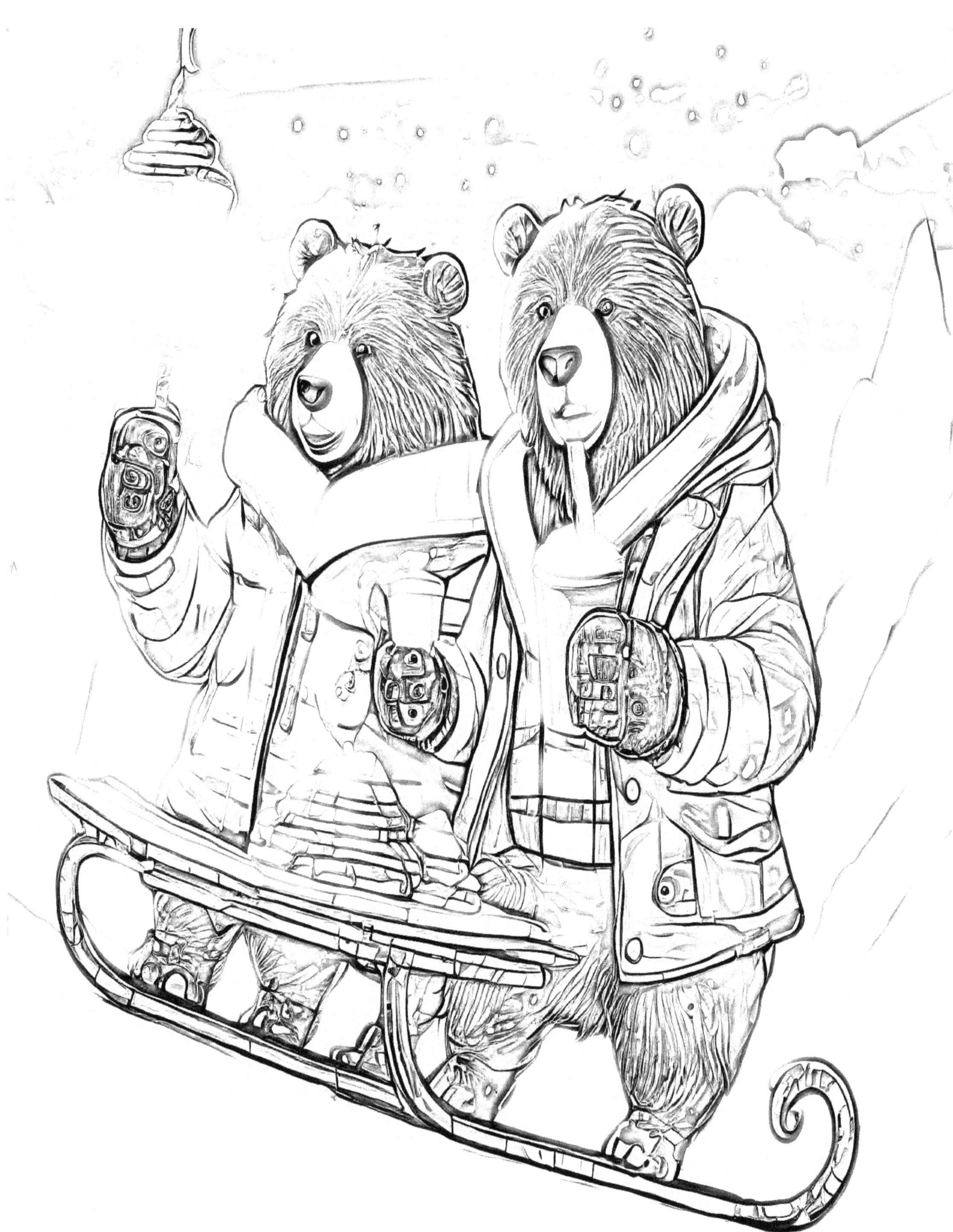

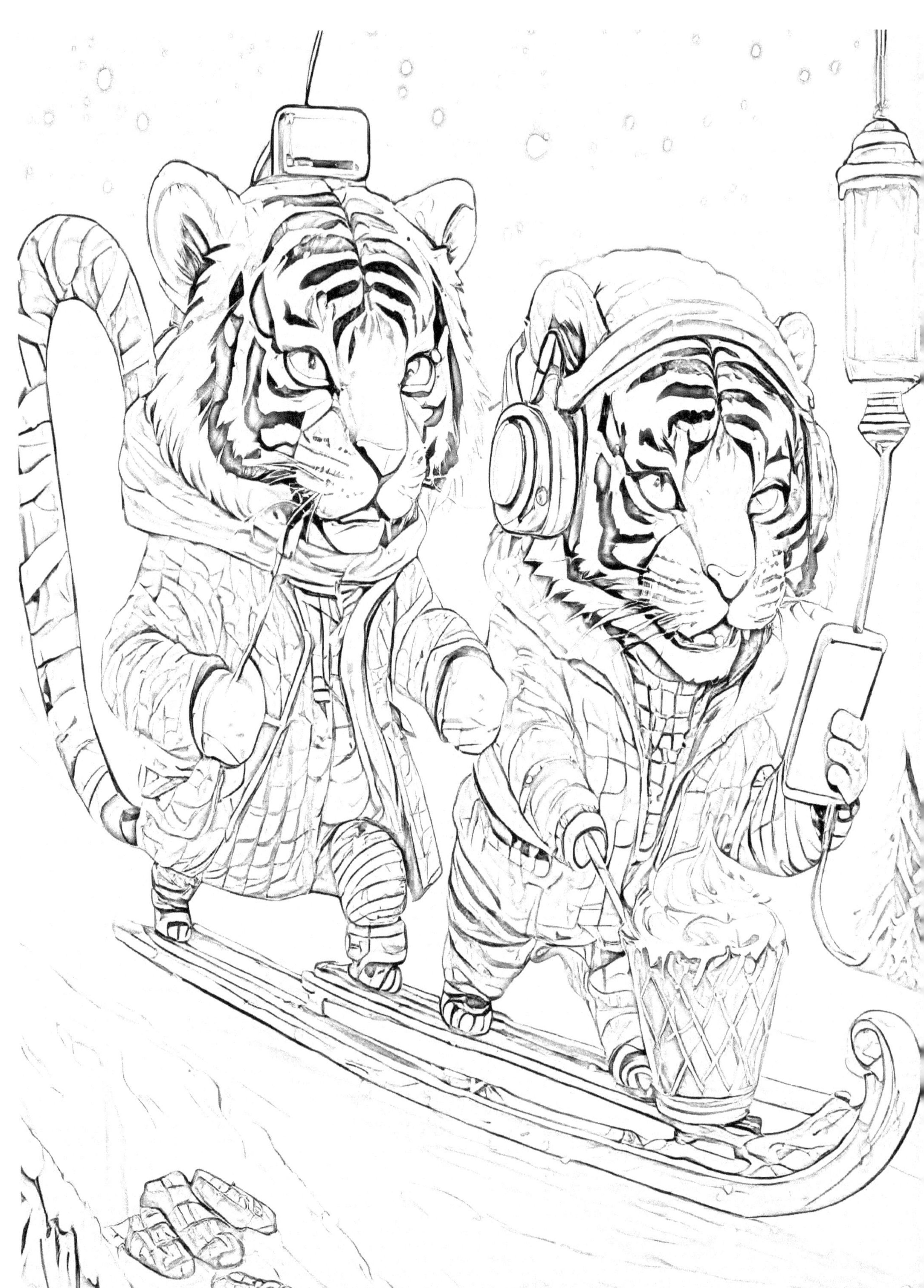

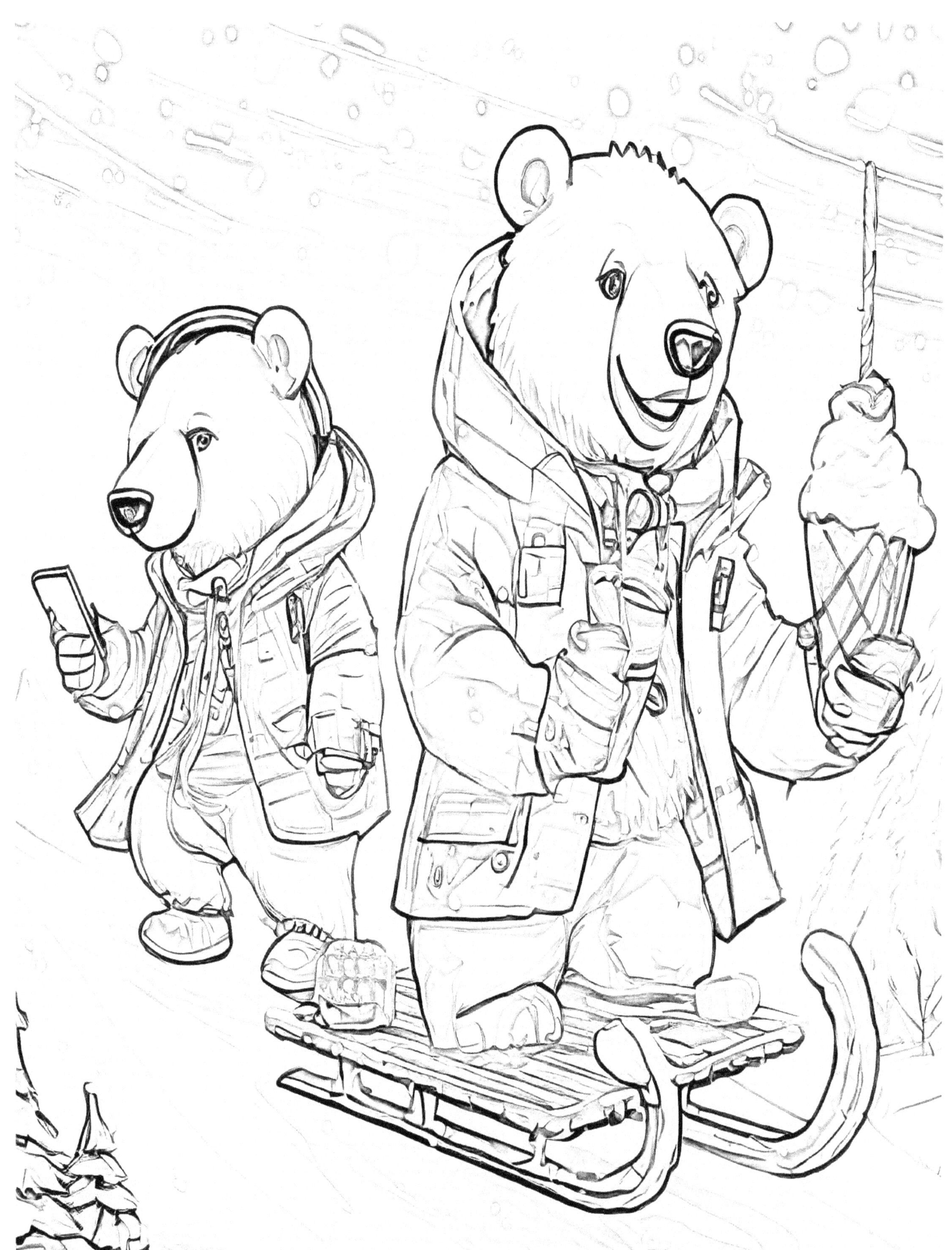

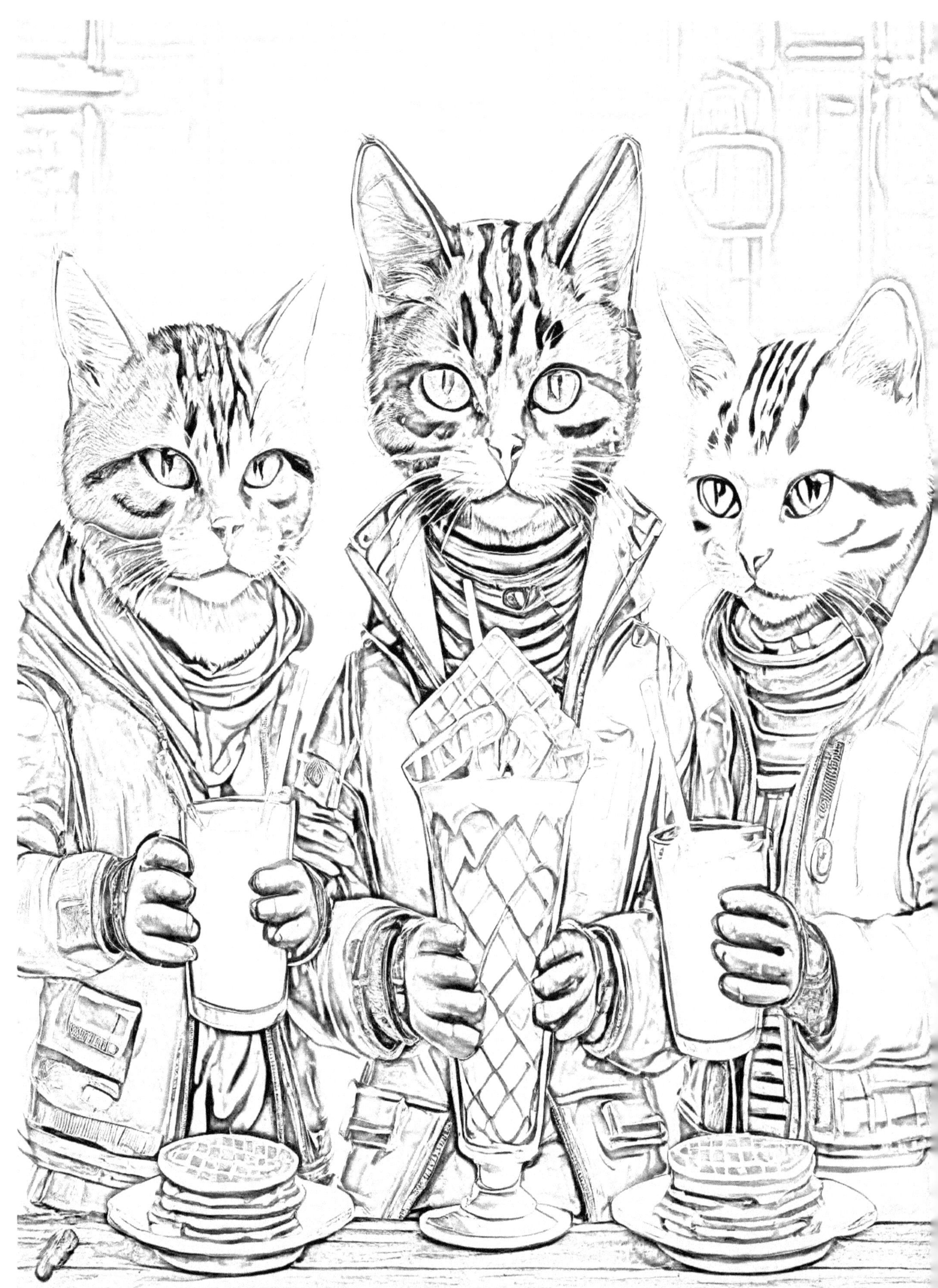

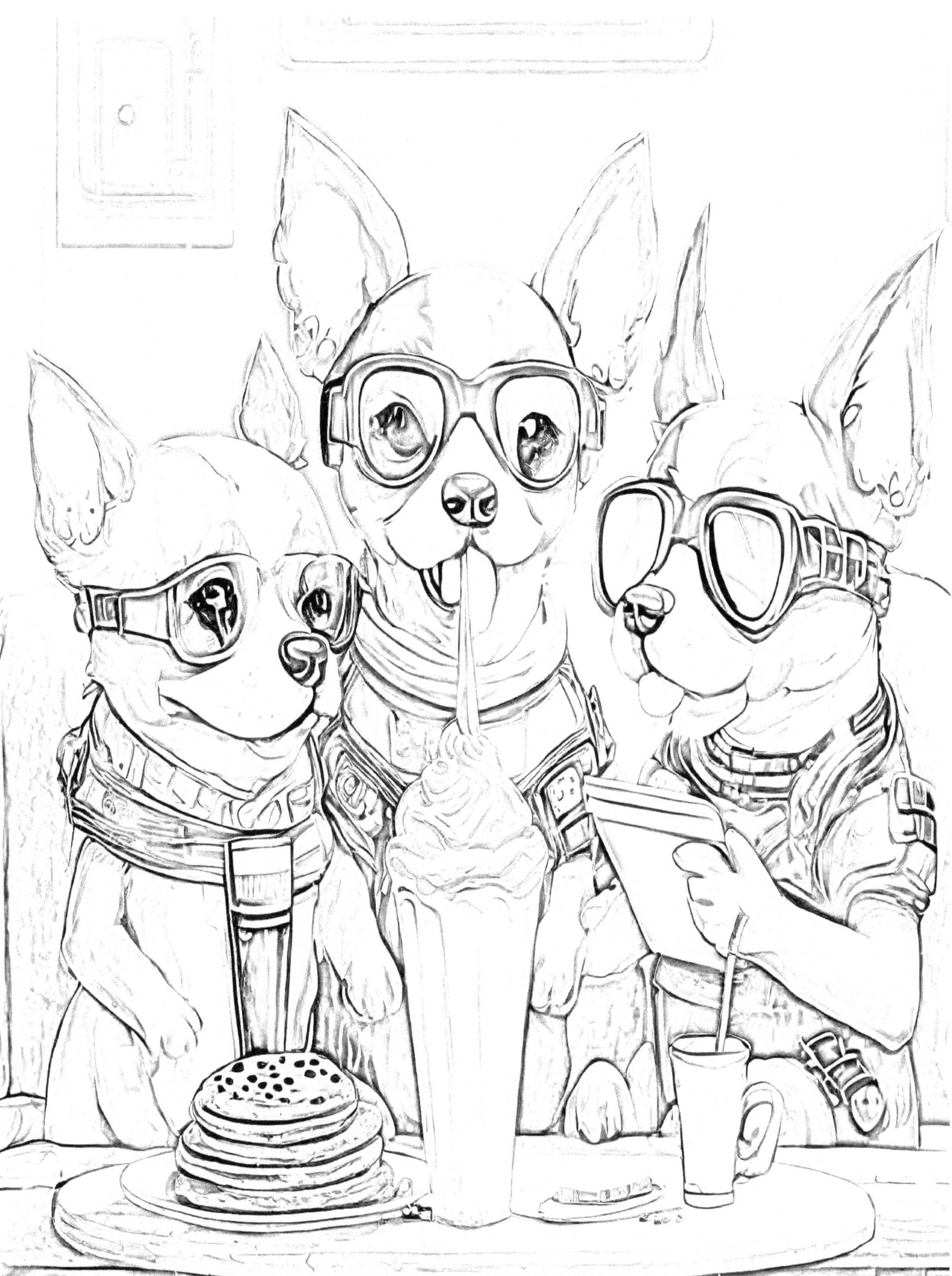

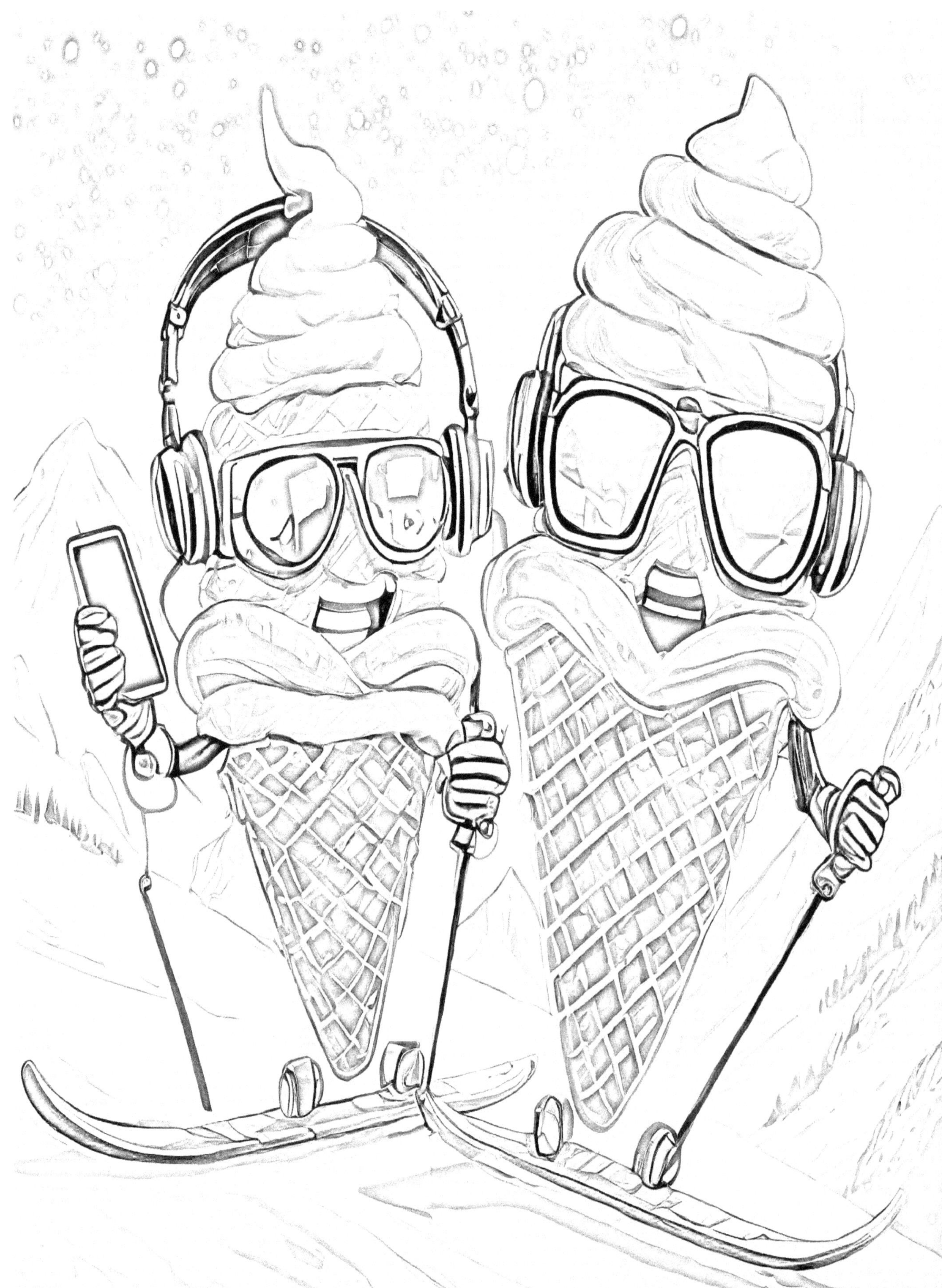

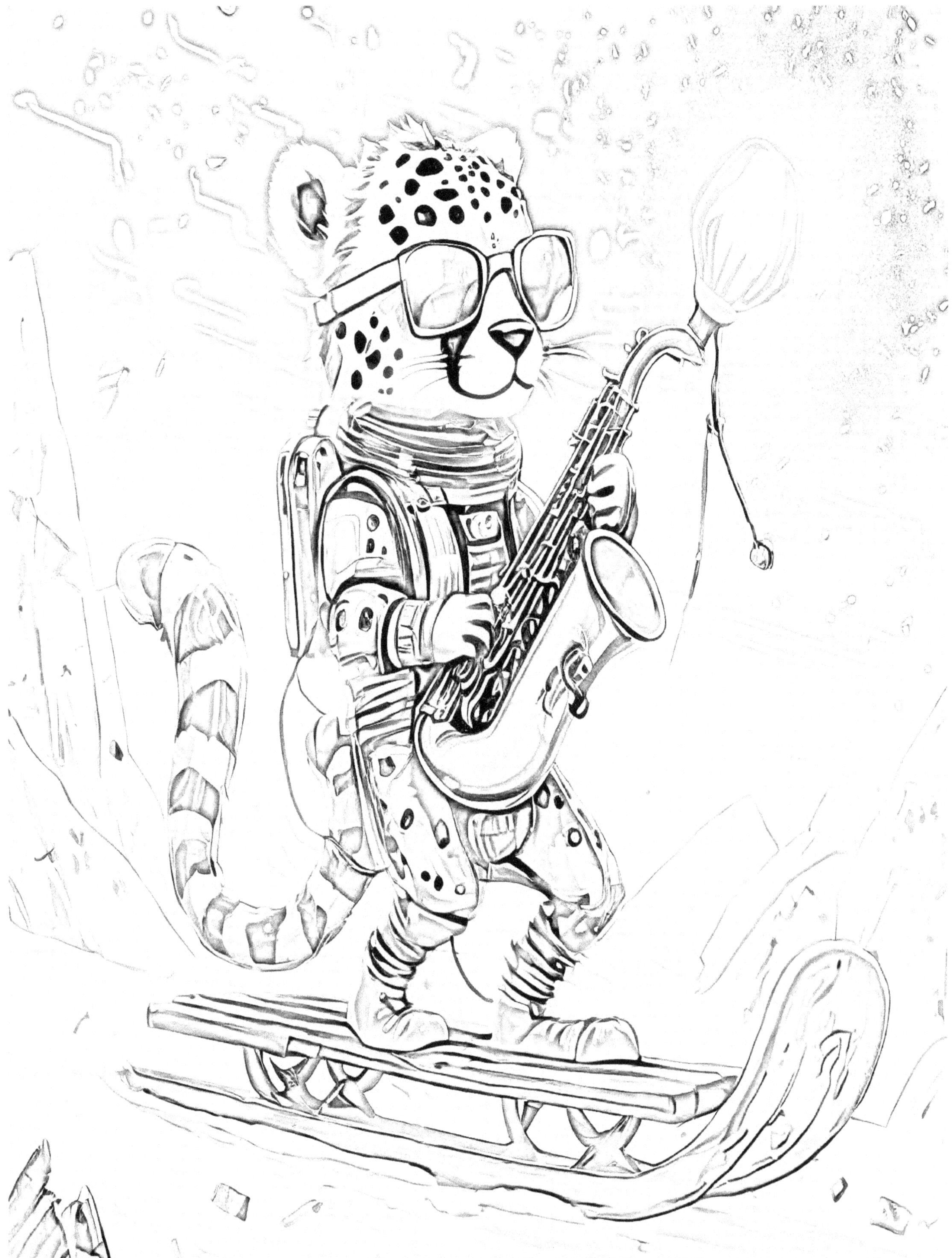

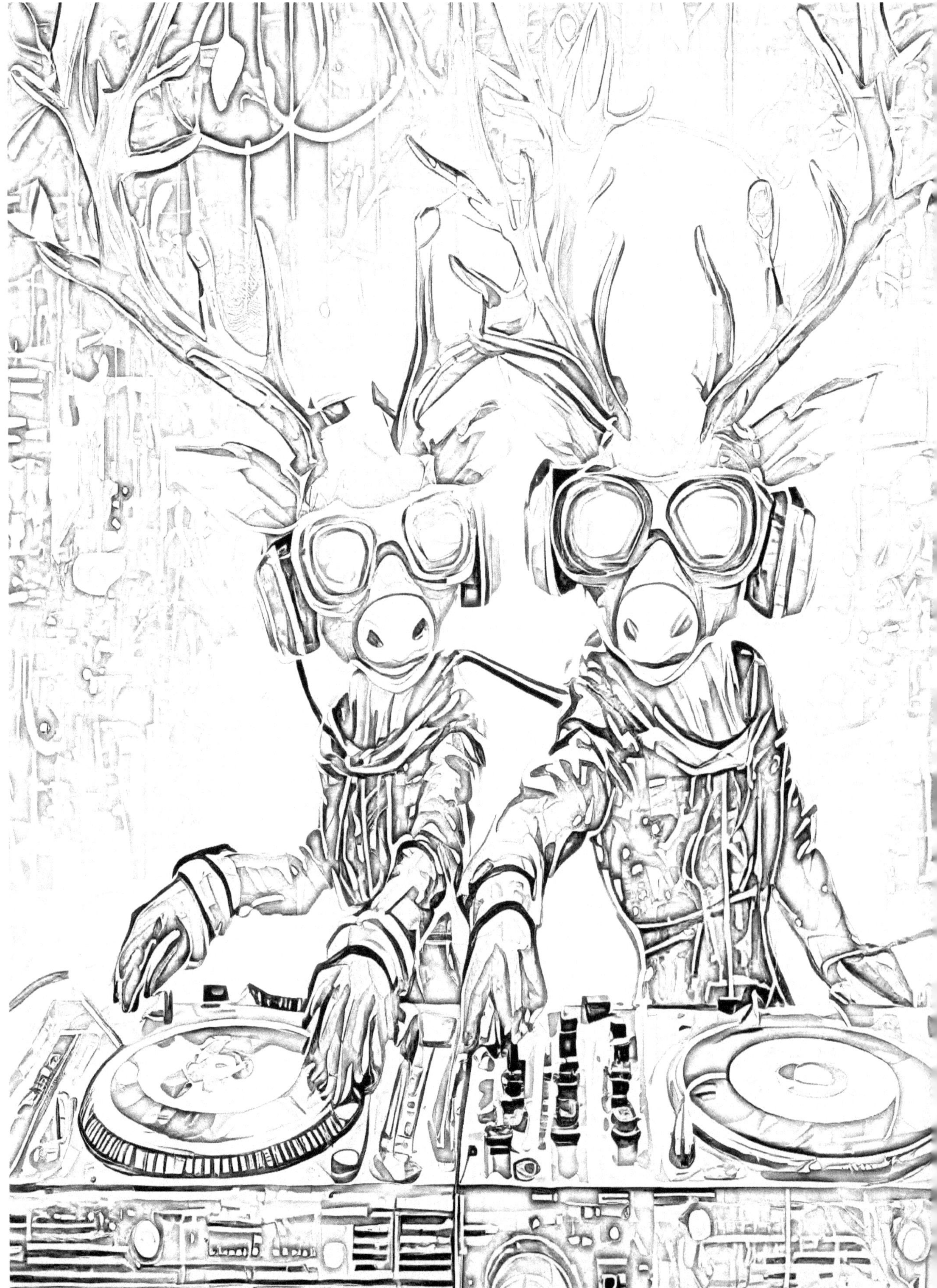

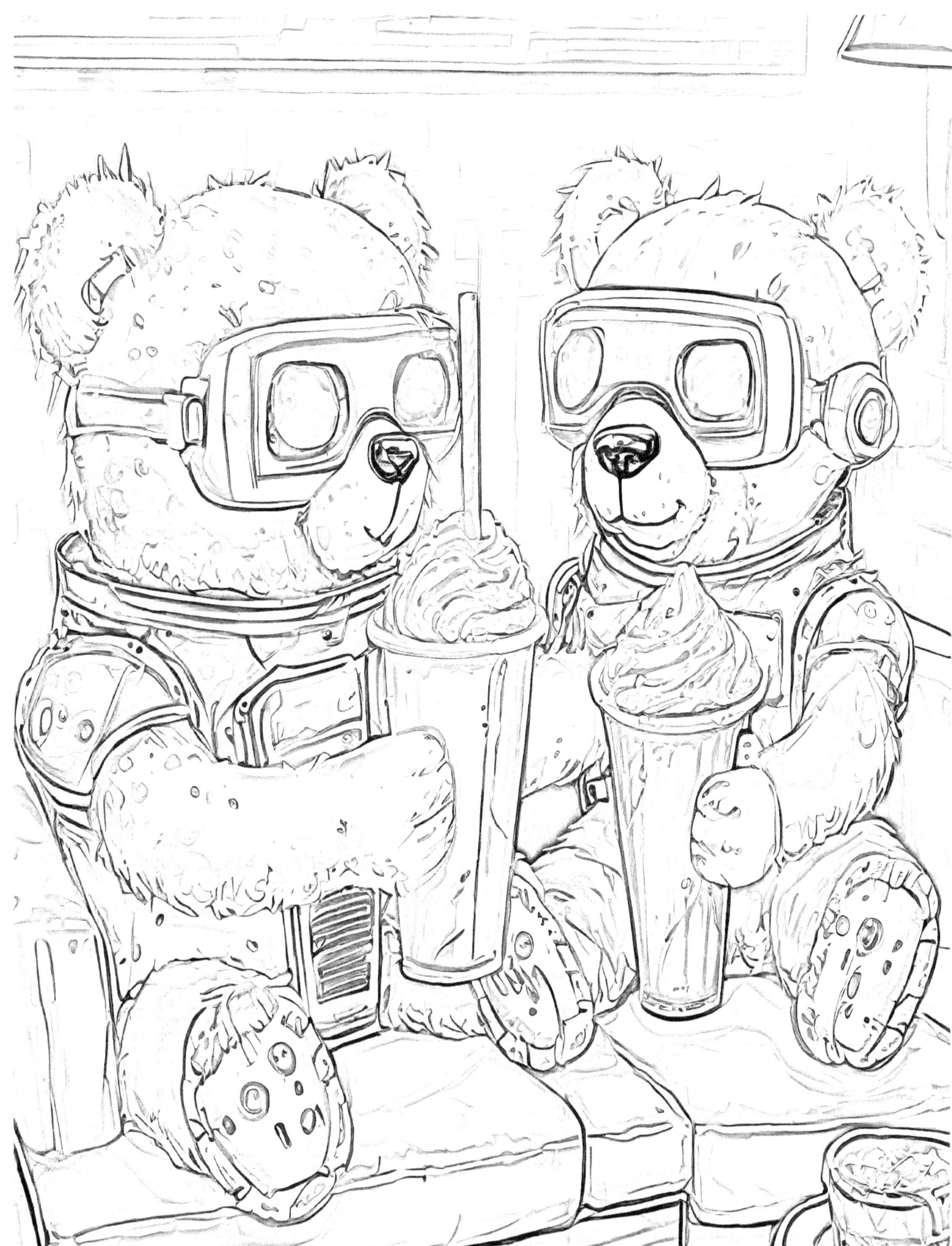

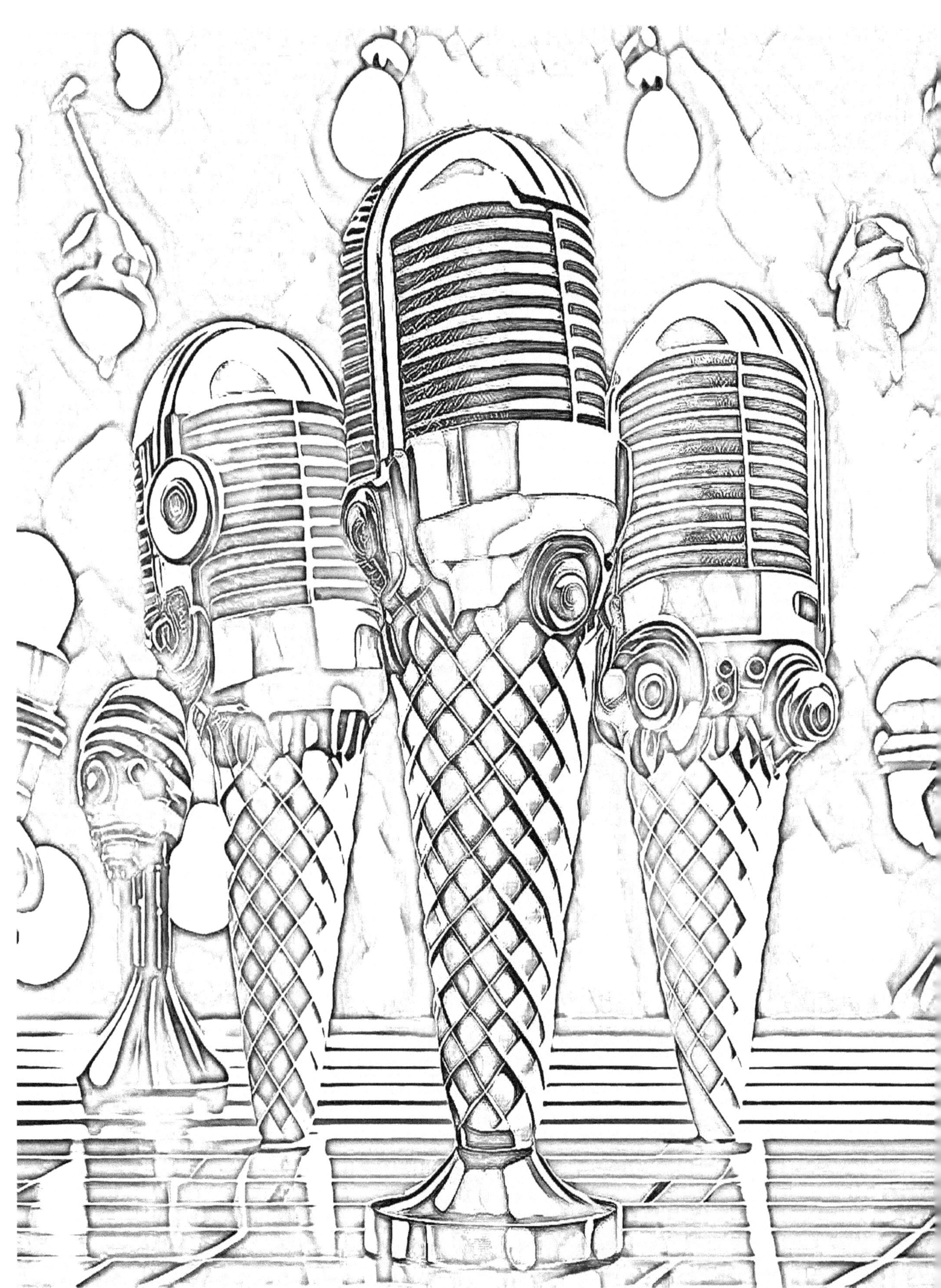

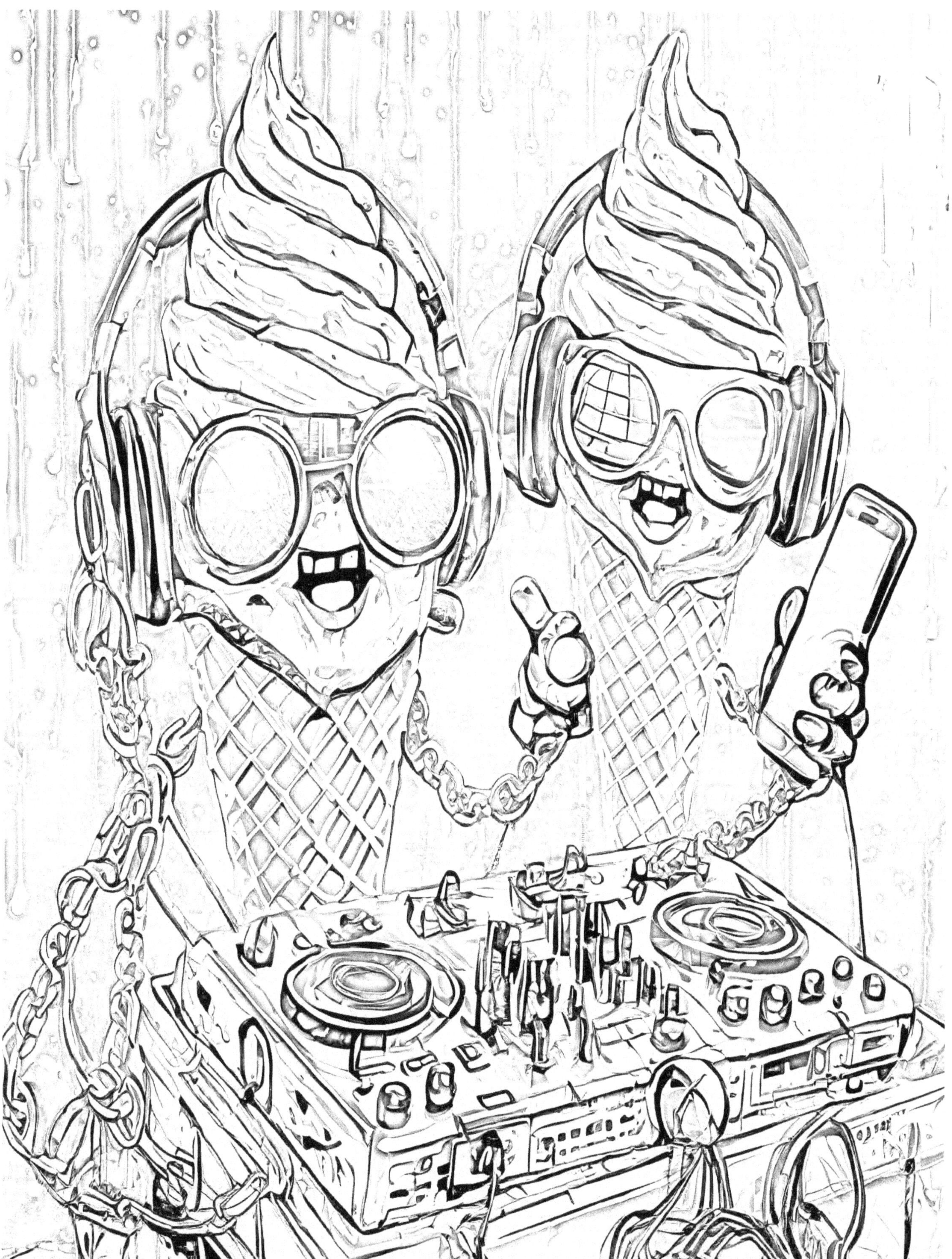

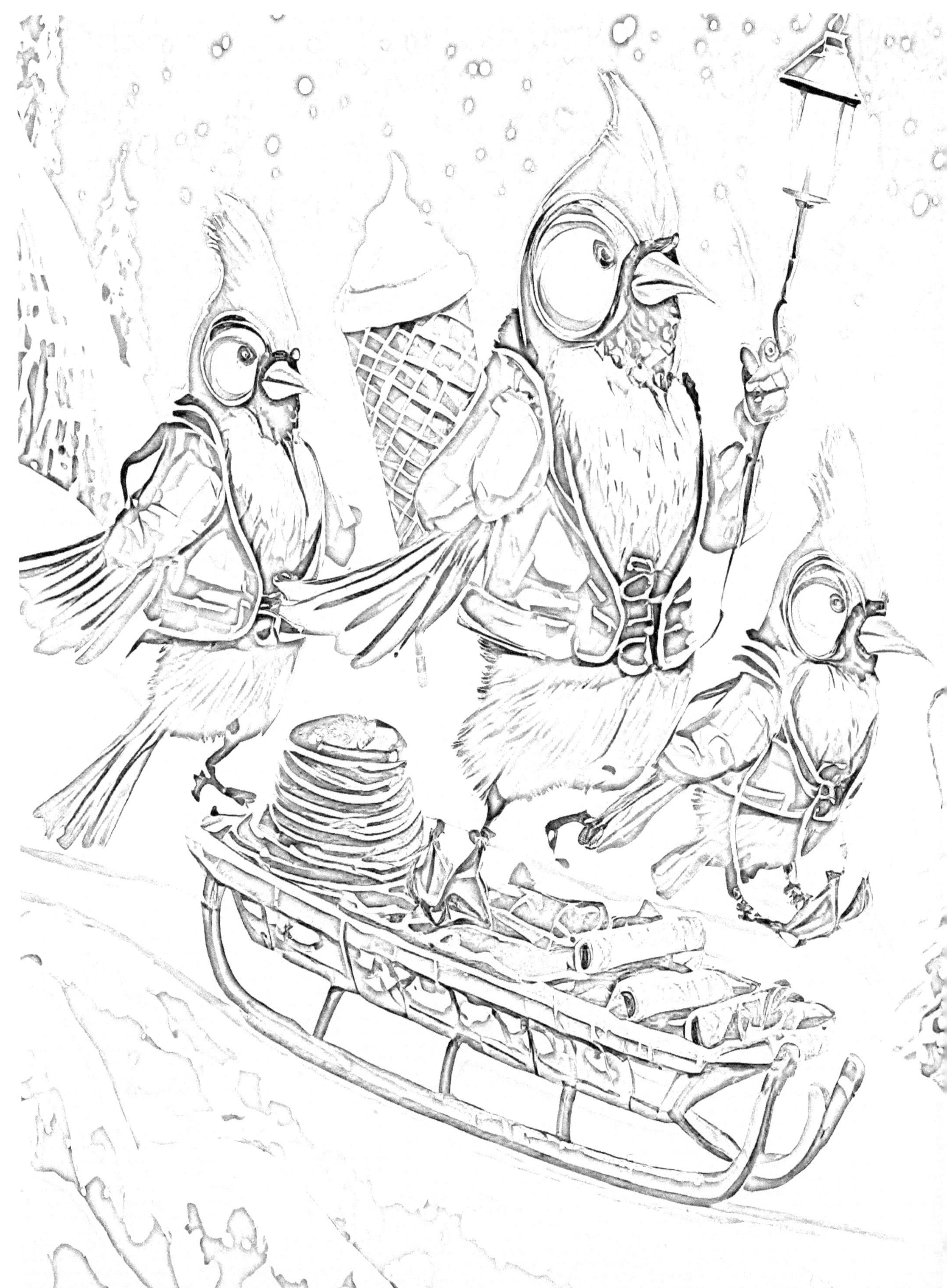

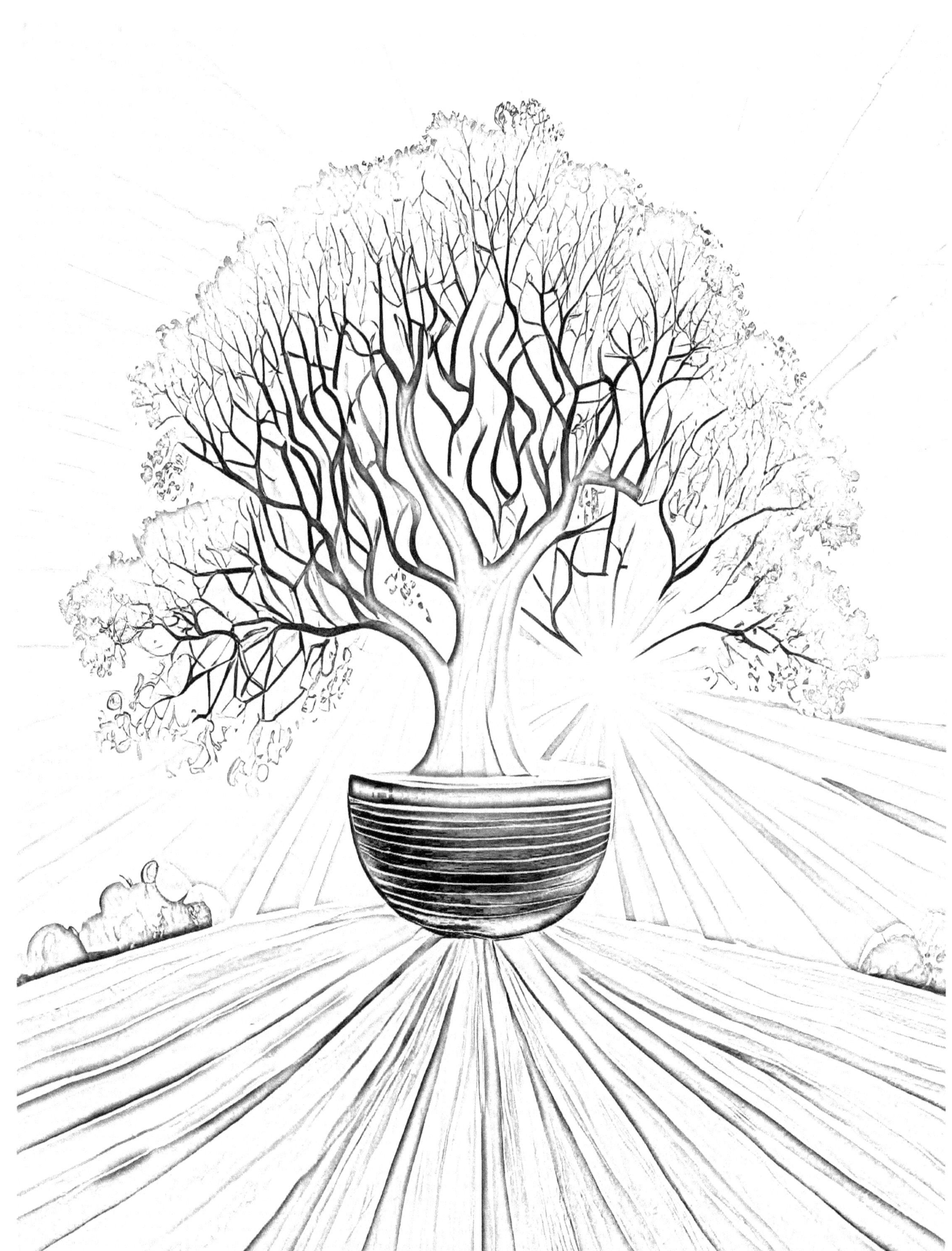

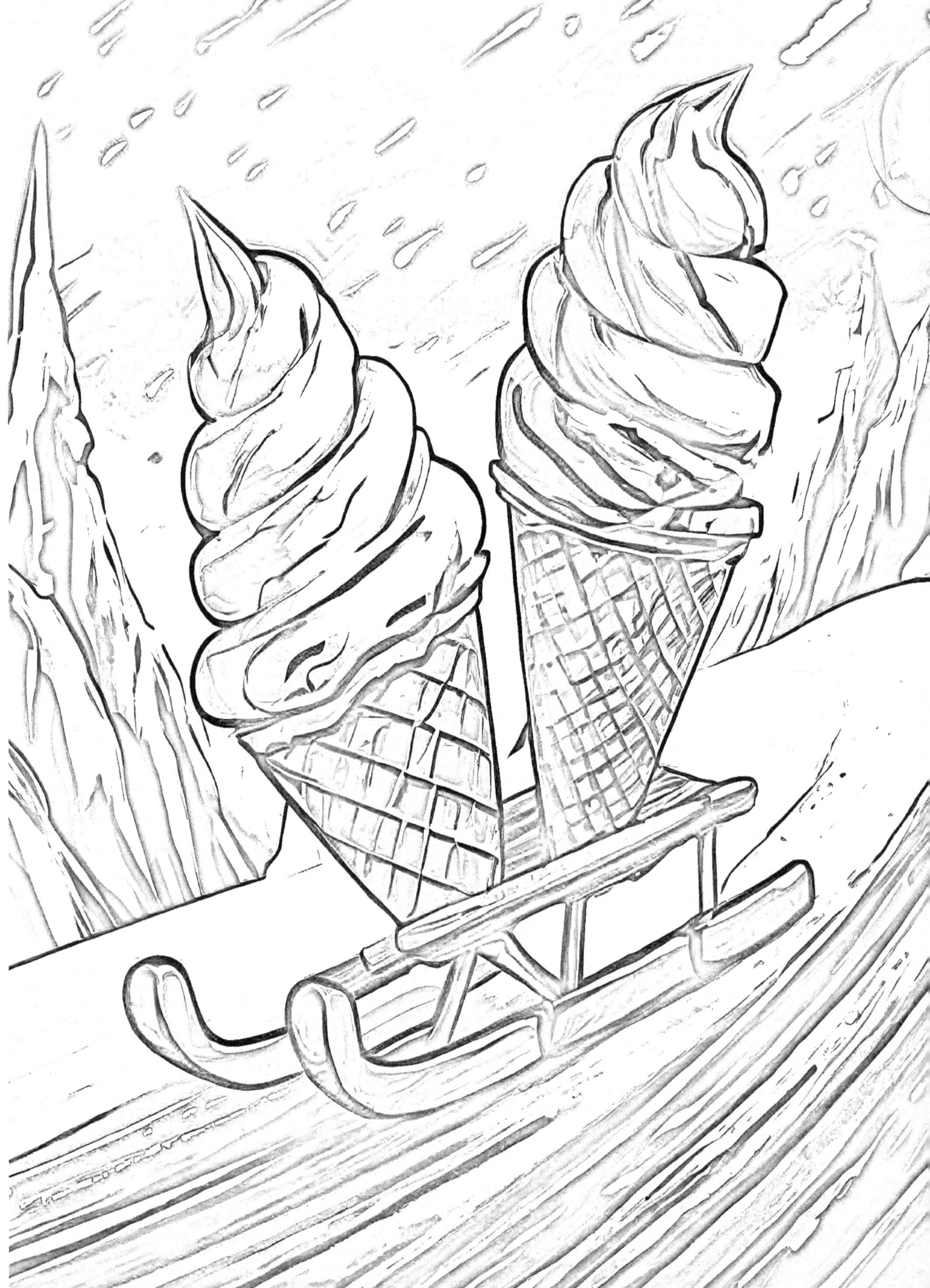

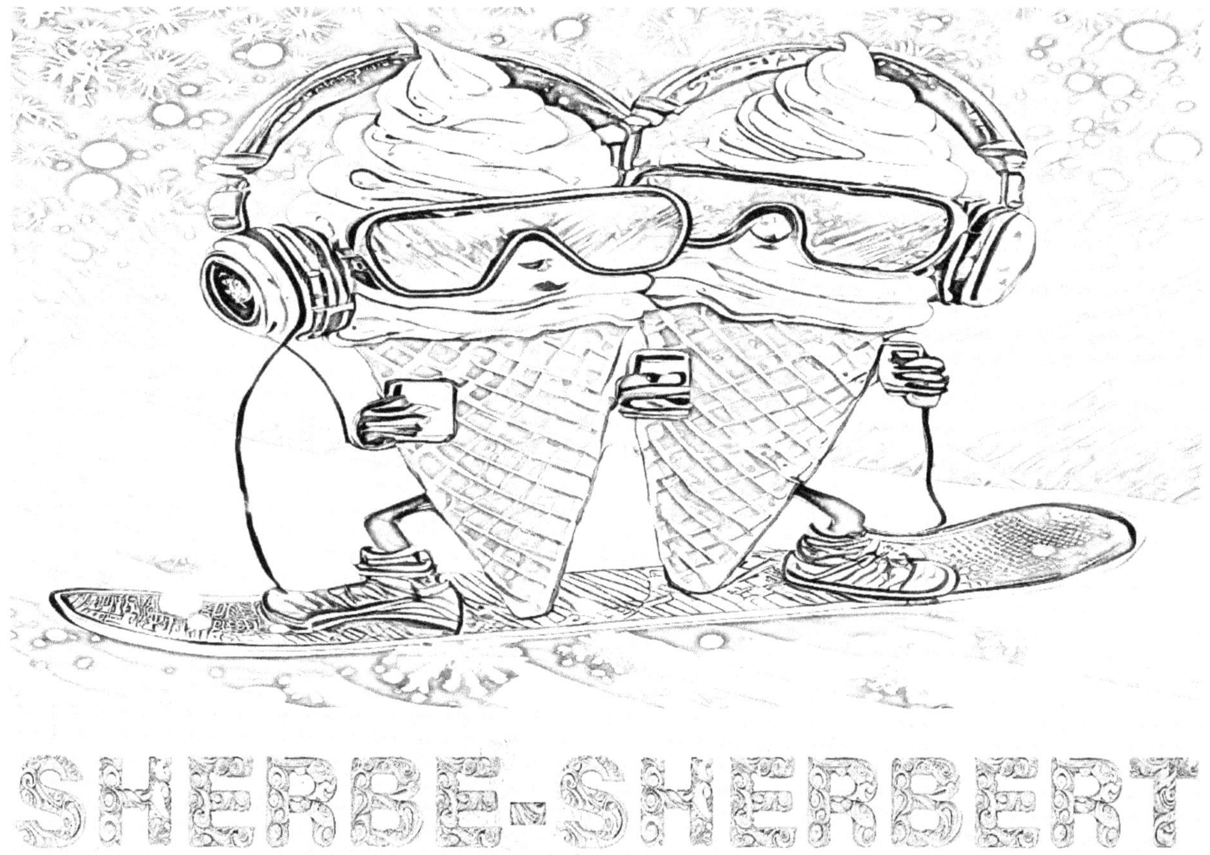

ISBN: 979-8-9902578-2-5

www.ingramcontent.com/pod-product-compliance
Lightning Source LLC
LaVergne TN
LVHW060641110826
845147LV00018B/1019

* 9 7 9 8 9 9 0 2 5 7 8 2 5 *